BEST OF ALL

Main Dish Salads

CAROLINE BEST

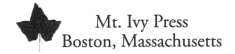

Mt. Ivy Press
Boston, Massachusetts

© Copyright 1994
by Mt. Ivy Press
All rights reserved

First Edition Published 1994

Design: BECKdesigns

Printed in U.S.A.

ISBN 0-9635257-1-9

Library of Congress Catalog Card Number 93-80901

Mt. Ivy Press, Inc.
P.O. Box 142
Boston, MA 02258

on the cover

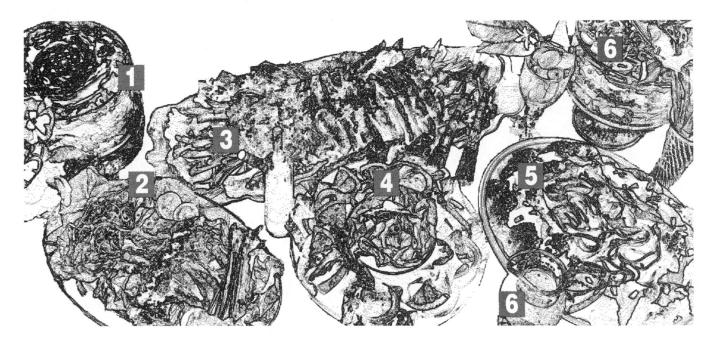

table of contents

v

the seven essential virtues of a "Best Recipe"

Call me driven or compulsive or whatever. In my quarter century in the kitchen I've taken on a mission of searching for "best recipes" — not just nice or pleasant dishes but the Best of All of a particular type. Take potato salad. Have you ever considered what would be the best version that doesn't use mayonnaise? Well, I have and therein lies my compulsive side but we'll get to that recipe later. Meanwhile, I'd like to share with you my checklist for a top rating. To be The Best a recipe must be...

1 **DELICIOUS** Not surprisingly my number one criterion for a best recipe is that it must produce a dish that tastes absolutely wonderful. Even if it's just egg salad, it should be the freshest tasting, the lightest textured. It should also be the brightest yellow meaning the eggs were not over-cooked and gray around the yolks. Which leads to number two.

2 **BEAUTIFUL** Since food appeals to our eyes as well as our taste buds, the dish must look appetizing. It should make your mouth water. Cooks today are especially conscious of presentation, and that's great. But, personally, I don't care for the "food stylist" approach that treats a plate as a canvas and food as paints. Those too precisely composed, artificial dishes one sees frequently in food publications strike me as too much of a good thing.

I like food to look like food. The artistry of the cook should be casual and appropriate not obvious and forced. For instance, it's currently fashionable to serve little dabs of food in little pools of sauce surrounded by a few leaves on big plates. But this just doesn't work for either dieters or big eaters. People counting calories dread leaving the table hungry. Dabs, dribbles, sprigs and exposed china send the wrong message no matter how artful the arrangement. Abundance, I believe, is always welcome at any table. Lots of colorful veggies cut in interesting ways (shredded, julienned or paper-thin) add "abbondanza" without calories.

1

NOVEL We all tend to tire of the same ol' thing; therefore, a best recipe should produce a dish that's a bit unexpected, a little surprising. Novelty, however, should not be achieved without regard to taste. Take ice cream, for instance. Avocado ice cream is certainly more unusual than strawberry, but it doesn't taste as good. So why bother?

Things unexpected are tricky because most of us aren't up for eating anything that we perceive as "weird." As a caterer, I learned that most people prefer foods that are basically familiar, but with a twist that provides a little flair. At one time shark was a bit too much of a twist on swordfish (which it closely resembles) to be a good choice for, say, a wedding rehearsal dinner. Don't ask how I know this. It's probably not okay even today.

 SHORT A perfect recipe should contain a short to moderate number of ingredients, not a list as long as a column in the phone book.

 EASY It must not be so exotic or far-out that we don't have the ingredients on hand, can't get them easily, or need to learn a complicated new skill to prepare them.

 FAST These first five criteria alone still leave a multitude of possible "best recipes" if we all had unlimited time to spend in the kitchen. But the sixth narrows the field drastically: The recipe must be relatively quick to prepare. If it has to chill or bake for a long time without supervision, that's okay so long as we do not have to be there working on it.

7 MORE THAN THE SUM OF ITS PARTS A recipe that meets all these criteria produces a dish that is much more than the sum of its parts. Precious few recipes achieve this level. I've undoubtedly tossed out 100 recipes for every one I've tucked in my files, and of the "keeps" relatively few stand out as Perfect Tens. That's why I've said for years that if the house caught fire I'd save my children first, my jewelry second, and my recipe files third. My husband? He's capable of getting out by himself!

I've taken a little poll over the years on the subject of cook books: How many people read cook books in bed? Countless, even men. How many people buy cookbooks on impulse? Just about every woman I know, few men. How many good recipes do you need from a cook book to feel that you didn't waste your money? The average answer was three, but many people (including Julia Child, I'm told) answer one! My own answer: two.

Well, that's a pretty low standard and I'm not going to adhere to it in this cook book. All the recipes in here are good. You may like some better than others but there are no duds invented at the last minute as fillers. There are no self-conscious arty creations featuring things like garlic and vanilla together for cutting-edge trendiness. These are best recipes gleaned from hundreds of books and magazines, swapped with scores of wonderful cooks — professionals, friends and family — and refined by many repetitions.

This is not a definitive work on salads. I have not attempted to be scholarly or thorough. You will notice a preponderance of Thai and Middle Eastern dishes and salmon – all favorites of mine. This book is more of a rambling culinary memoir for me. Every recipe has a story. Some stories are worth the telling, some not. But all the recipes are worth trying. By the way, see page 21 for that best potato salad that doesn't contain mayonnaise.

happy cooking!

a few of my favorite kitchen gadgets & appliances

BY A CERTAIN AGE, I've heard it said, if you don't already have it, you don't need it — "it" being anything you don't already have. For the most part, I'm at that stage. But 'twas not always so. I once had a bumper sticker that proclaimed "I brake for tag sales." Now on those infrequent occasions when I do stop for a tag sale, at the precise instant that some thing-a-majig catches my fancy, a little voice whispers three practical questions:

"Where will you store it?"

"How often will you use it?"

"Who's going to dust it?"

It is incomprehensible to me that one of the most requested bridal gifts is a bread machine. If you're going to be so earthy-crunchy that you bake your own bread, what's wrong with doing it the old-fashioned way? Most of the joy of making bread is in the feel of the dough. Mixing and kneading dough by hand reminds us that yeast is actually alive. A plump loaf just placed in its pan for a final rising feels like a baby's fanny — same springiness, same warmth, and same colors as human skin, from white to pumpernickel and all shades in between. Aside from completely removing the baker from the true joys of making bread, a bread machine fails to adequately answer the three practical questions mentioned above.

I once wrote an article for which I interviewed a number of professional chefs on how they had set up their home kitchens. One told me he disliked cabinets. "My pots and pans are the tools of my trade," he told me. "I like them out in the open, on display. Besides, it's time-consuming and inconvenient to dig around in a dark cabinet looking for a particular piece of equipment." At home as at work all his pots, pans, ladles and spatulas were hung from racks within easy reach. This doesn't work if your utensils are not in constant use, however, because they get greasy and dusty out in the open.

People who cook in professional kitchens grow accustomed to a degree of serviceability and convenience that many domestic cooks have not experienced. I have fine-tuned my home kitchen over many years. Here are some of the kitchen appliances and tools I find indispensable. Even if you are at "that stage," I recommend the following:

An in-sink **boiling water dispenser** probably seems frivolous. In fact, one of the chefs in my above mentioned article told me she was planning to get one of these at her next kitchen renovation. When I did my kitchen over, I remembered her idea and ordered one for myself. It's so handy for making a quick cup of herb tea or filling a pot to boil spaghetti.

A small **book rack** is so useful in a kitchen. I have about 200 cookbooks but, of course, I only use a handful at any one time. These sit in a corner in a nice little rack that I appropriated from my son when he graduated from college and didn't need it anymore.

A **bread box and a cookie jar** can add style to a kitchen as well as convenience. My breadbox is a vintage enameled beauty I found in an antique store. I have a number of cookie jars. One of my favorites is lovely painted tinware, with the soft patina that only time can bestow. I also have pottery cookie jars — one in the shape of a fat pig, another a dapper cat in a hat, another a wily fox. Family and close friends make a bee-line for the cookie jar as soon as they come in the house.

Grilling is the big thing these days. Everyone loves the taste of grilled meats, fish and vegetables. A cook top or range with a **built-in grill** allows you to enjoy outdoors-y flavors all year 'round. My grill has a layer of lava stones suspended over the gas flame. Those rocks are what make the food taste good. Most people don't realize that the characteristic grilled flavor we all love comes not from charcoal but from dripping fat and juices hitting the heat source, vaporizing, rising as smoke and "basting" the meat. To increase the smoky taste, make a flat foil packet of hickory or mesquite chips, poke holes in the top of the foil, lay the packets on the pre-heated coals and set the rack on top. Place the food on the rack and drape a foil tent over the the grill to trap the smoke. It's not necessary to soak wood chips in water before using them; in fact, this just delays the smoke. I've seen directions for soaking wood chips in wine…a waste of good wine as the flavor will not rise in the smoke. (Nor does steaming over wine impart any wine flavor, by the way.)

A **bulletin strip** is a handy device. It's a strip of cork 2 inches wide and in varying lengths that mounts anywhere by means of sticky tabs or screws. I have mine on the refrigerator door but it could also go on a cabinet door. A few tacks is all it takes to affix a small calendar, the grocery list, a recipe, or a reminder where they can't be overlooked. I got mine from an office supply discount store for under $10.

A **citrus zester** is a small tool with tiny sharp-edged holes in one end that peel thin threads from the rind of a lemon or orange. The first zester I owned was so poorly made that it didn't make threads at all. I thought something was wrong with me that I couldn't get it to work. A better model (still under $5) still works beautifully after years of use. I love tossing long threads of lemon rind on top of salmon steaks, into gin and tonics, over sorbet, around lemon pound cake. A zester instantly makes anyone look like a real pro in the kitchen.

insulated cookie sheets are relatively new on the market. They consist of two layers of aluminum with an air space trapped between. Cookies on the lower shelf of the oven won't burn on their bottoms and those at the edge of the pan cook almost as slowly as those in the center. These cookie sheets cost about twice as much as the single-layer pans but they pay for themselves in unburned cookies.

knife rack or knife magnet There are at least two better ways to store knives than keeping them in a drawer, providing you don't have curious young children. If you have room near your work surface, a wood or marble block with slots in it to hold them works nicely. My favorite, however, is a magnetic strip that screws to the side of a cabinet. The magnet holds the knives securely by their blades and allows you to see just the one you need.

I have a big, commercial strength Cuisinart, but not a day goes by that I don't use my **little food processor.** The bowl holds just about two cups. It's the perfect size to mince onions, chop eggs for egg salad, grate cheese, purée salsa, or grind nuts for cookies. The one I have is a Sunbeam Oskar but there are a number of other good brands on the market.

An in-sink **liquid detergent dispenser** may sound silly but when I did my kitchen over I hunted for a sink that had an extra opening by the faucet to accommodate this little squirter. It's so nice to be able to quickly grab a dab of detergent without having to keep a messy bottle out in the open.

A **mandoline** is an inexpensive vegetable slicer, a slab about 5"x14" with an embedded blade. This gizmo can turn a whole potato into a pile of transparently thin slices for Potatoes Caroline (see Go-Withs) in a minute. This thinness is virtually impossible to achieve with a knife unless you are one of those unbelievable Samurai chefs who perform grillside in Japanese restaurants.

Somehow the flavor of many vegetables is enhanced by being cut very thin. Cucumber salad, for instance, definitely tastes better when the slices are like paper, also steamed carrots. You can make a garnish of onion "strings", tissue-thin slices of onion quickly deep-fried until rich brown. Some mandolines have changeable blades that produce varying thickness, cut French fry-type pieces and julienne. You can find a mandloline in a discount store for under $10 or in a kitchen shop for about $20.

My **microwave** is constantly in use. I prefer the smallest size because I almost never use mine to prepare dishes from scratch. A small microwave takes little counter space and is terrific for reheating leftovers, melting butter, warming tepid coffee or doing any other menial chore without dirtying a pan.

There are very few dishes that don't start out by cooking onion or garlic in a bit of oil. That's why **oil cans** are a real convenience. I have two by the cooktop, one for peanut oil and one for olive oil, the two kinds I use most frequently. Each can holds less than 2 cups, has a long narrow spout that pours a thin slow stream allowing me control. Specialty cooking shops and mail order catalogs offer a variety of models.

recipe holder Have you ever gotten half way through a dish and not been able to find a recipe? You have to stop what you're doing and move every towel, can and bowl on the counter before it turns up in the floor where it fell. Sometimes it's just the littlest things that make life less frustrating. There are any number of ingenious devices that hold a recipe while you are cooking from it. My mother has one that she got at a country fair that's made with a simple spring clothespin in a little stand. Mine is a tall metal stand that was used in a hotel banquet room to hold table placards. I couldn't cook without it.

I use my **salad spinner** to wash all kinds of vegetables, not just lettuce. With so much concern about lingering agricultural pesticides these days this kitchen item has real health value. The best kind has three pieces: a large plastic bowl, a plastic basket that fits inside it and a lid. Place vegetables like beans, broccoli or spinach in the basket, set the basket into its bowl and fill to the brim with several changes of water, lifting out the basket after each fill. A few turns on the crank and the vegetables are almost dry.

I haven't used a salt shaker in years. Instead I keep salt in a small redwood **salt box** with its own wooden spoon. It's easier to see how much I'm adding and there's nothing to clog. I also have a very tall wooden **peppermill**, the kind a waiter flourishes over your salad in fancy restaurants. Because of its size, it never gets lost in the flurry.

Spoon jars save time and aggravation. On the counter by the cooktop I keep two pottery crocks containing spatulas, ladles, whisks and wooden spoons that I use most frequently. Everything is nearby and in sight when I need it in a hurry.

A **spoon rest** helps to keep mess down around the cooking area. Although any saucer will do, I have two decorative spoon rests — one in the shape of an artichoke, the other, a stalk of celery. While one is in the dishwasher I use the other.

Stainless steel roasting pans are the best. They cook more evenly, but best of all, they clean easily without a lot of scouring and scrubbing. With a little care, they will never get that black, burnt grease coating at the edges and on the bottom that inevitably occurs with aluminum pans.

A **thermometer**, of the instant read variety, is very handy for times when you just can't screw up — poaching a whole salmon or grilling an entire fillet of beef. The trick with this type of thermometer is to test frequently as the dish nears doneness. Plunge the thermometer deep into the meat or fish — at least half the length of the stem. If just the tip is embedded the temperature reading will be lower than it really is. If necessary, slide the thermometer in on a long horizontal.

Professional kitchens usually don't have the advantage of cabinets over the counters as do most home kitchens. Under-cabinet space can be useful in many ways. I love my **under-cabinet fluorescent lights** which shed extra light on my work areas and give the kitchen a lovely indirect glow when the overhead lights are turned off. In order to keep clutter off the counter tops I have installed an **under-cabinet continuous clean toaster oven** made by Black and Decker. I just love this little appliance and use it several times a day. Besides making toast, it can bake small potatoes in a jiffy, melt cheese sandwiches, brown the top of a casserole, or any number of other odd jobs. It uses less electricity than my big oven and doesn't heat up the whole kitchen. I long ago gave away my regular toaster — it's too limited in function to waste space on. Also in that space is my **under-cabinet electric can opener** (Black and Decker again), that has a detachable cutter that can be cleaned in the dishwasher. I believe that the only time one should open cans by hand is when on a camping trip.

wide spatula This tool is essential for turning large delicate things such as a whole fish or big pancakes.

the pantry shelf

There's been something of a revolt against commercial foods lately. The additives, the salt, the hidden fats, the whole idea of foods made not in a kitchen but in a factory have fueled suspicions concerning things that come in cans and boxes. While some of this is justified, the pendulum may have swung too far when a perfectly good product is tarred with the same brush that condemns brilliant orange, artificially-flavored, saturated fat-soaked snack products.

Over the years, I have tried thousands of products but certain items have become staples. Here are some thoughts on the subject of ingredients.

asian seasonings When Western cooks go into an Asian market they initially feel acute culture shock. The dazzling array of strange ingredients — packets of dried shrimp, cans of pickled turnips, tapioca flour, bean paste, noodles of every size and shape — can be overwhelming. Despite the endless variety, just a few items can get you going cooking Chinese, Thai or other Asian cuisines.

If you are just starting out stocking your larder here are the basics: Buy all-purpose Chinese-style white rice in bulk. Small shops generally buy rice in huge quantities and put up smaller packages for their customers. You'll also need peanut oil; the gallon size is not too big if you want to do some frying. For seasonings, soy sauce, of course, is number one. Buy a good-size bottle of light soy (paler color, thinner, less salty) for seafood and chicken dishes. For an all-purpose soy, Kikkoman is my favorite. Other basics: sesame oil, chili paste, oyster sauce, hoisin sauce, fish sauce, dry black mushrooms, hot oil, five spice powder and rice vinegar will cover most dishes with the addition of fresh items such as garlic, ginger, coriander, chilies and onions. For Thai cooking, throw in a few cans of coconut milk. Add some noodles: dried mung bean or cellophane noodles in various widths, rice noodles, and fresh wheat flour noodles from the refrigerator case. Experiment a bit with wrappers. Wonton wrappers, also found in the refrigerator case, can be fried and sprinkled with cinnamon and sugar, a treat for the kids. Another wrapper, big dried rice paper disks can be dunked in water, then set between damp paper towels to soften. For an unusual presentation fill these with a mixture of bean sprouts, chopped scallion, cooked rice and shrimp and tie the bundles with a strip of scallion cord, Top with Vietnamese Dressing, page 145.

A trip to an Asian market can open a whole new world. If you go to a one that primarily serves an ethnic clientele, you will be amazed at how small you bill will be.

bacon The best bacon comes from a smokehouse, not the grocery store. Smokehouse bacon is so flavorful that I use it as a seasoning. Check out your area for a local smokehouse or order from a mail order company (there are sometimes ads for these in the back of cooking magazines.) The taste will tell you it's worth the extra time and cost. My favorite bacon comes from Harrington's of Vermont, Main Street, Richmond, VT 05477. Call (802) 434-4444 to place an order or request a catalog. The smell of Harrington's cob- and maplewood-smoked bacon cooking is on a par with the smell of good coffee grinding — It almost makes you swoon.

I have a couple of prepared products in mind that I want to defend. First, I find **biscuit mix** very handy as an ingredient in many dishes, some in the Go-Withs section of this book. The quickie quiches (see pages 133 and 142) that can be made with biscuit mix are not the same as the real thing but can be absolutely delicious in their own way. There are several brands of mix on the market and they seem to be interchangeable. Each box has recipes on the side for coffee cakes, muffins, waffles and many other uses for the mix. I use biscuit mix just to make biscuits (NO!) sometimes enhanced with grated cheese, bits of ham or bacon, or mashed sweet potatoes or squash in place of milk.

bouillon I always use homemade stock for soups but in other dishes, if I don't have homemade on hand, I rarely use canned broth. It seems wasteful to buy a great big metal can of something that is mostly water when bouillon cubes work as well in most cases. I always have several kinds of bouillon cubes and granules on hand. I use chicken bouillon granules (Wyler's) in place of salt in almost all cooked vegetables, sauces and gravies. I use beef granules in water for cooking artichokes. Knorr makes delicious fish-flavor bouillon cubes and also vegetarian-vegetable cubes. Goya makes an excellent ham-flavored cube that enhances bean soups and bitter greens such as broccoli rabe, mustard, kale or collards. To prepare greens, add a bit of minced bacon to the pan and a ham bouillon cube and steam in the wash water clinging to the leaves. Serve with a sprinkling of vinegar and hot sauce.

bread I almost never buy grocery store bread these days. It's never as good as bread from a bakery and certainly not as fresh. I've tracked down the best bakeries in my area. Whenever I have good bread in a restaurant I inquire where it comes from. Sometimes it's made on the premises, but usually the restaurant buys it from a wonderful bakery.

I do my bread shopping on Saturday, buying enough for the coming week from one or more sources. I freeze what will not be used immediately. Rye breads come from a Jewish bakery, sweet rolls and croissants from a French patisserie, and sour-dough, foccacia, and coarse textured white loaves at wholesale prices come from a bakery that primarily serves the restaurant trade. I also shop in Armenian markets for pita and lavash (another round flatbread) and lahmejeunes (a pizza like flat bread with a lamb and tomato topping.) Irish soda bread and bannocks (rolls) come from an Irish bakery. I never have to drive more than a few minutes to get the best and freshest breads in town. With a bit of snooping you, too, can find breads worthy of the name "the staff of life."

breadcrumbs are only as good as the bread they're made from. That's why I never throw away good bread that's gone stale. Instead I collect ends and pieces in a paper bag (not plastic so bread can dry without getting moldy) until I have a quart or so of dry crusts. These go into the processor to be ground into slightly coarse crumbs and stored in a jar with a tight lid. I don't season the crumbs until I use them, at which time I may add onion or garlic powder, herbs or Parmesan cheese. If you have not made your own breadcrumbs from good bread, you will be amazed at the difference. A chewy, crusty loaf produces the crunchiest crust for coating chicken breasts or topping a casserole.

butter Unsalted, a.k.a. "sweet," butter is the only kind I ever buy. When I want salt, I add it myself, thank you. Besides, salt helps to mask the flavor of old butter, allowing the producer to store it longer. Unsalted butter is likely to be a fresher product and its flavor is generally more delicate.

canned soups have taken a knock of late and this is another product I defend. Trendy food magazines never include recipes containing this ingredient. However unfashionable, I still like the creamed variety in casseroles or gravy or pasta sauce, or mixtures that get packed into ramekins and topped with buttered crumbs. Using canned cream of celery, chicken or mushroom soup saves the time and trouble of making a bechamel (milk-based white sauce.) Having made thousands of bechamels, I know from experience that cream soup is an excellent substitute, virtually indistinguishable from the scratch version (just omit added salt.)

I have fond memories of canned soups. As a child my favorite comfort food was buttered toast topped with a cheese rarebit containing but two ingredients: Velveeta cheese melted in canned undiluted tomato soup. Believe it or not, it's delicious.

ethnic markets There are any number of other ethnic markets right in our own neighborhoods that most of us never notice unless we happen to be of that ethnic group. For instance, there are two Armenian markets near my home where a shopper can ladle many kinds of olives and pickled vegetables from big wooden barrels, where the flat breads in the morning are still warm from the oven, where you can find bitter oranges to make real marmalade (navel oranges do *not* make marmalade,) where nuts of all kinds are sold from big bins, where feta cheese comes in six varieties and where the smell in the air is of spices and breads and good eating. It is a reminder of how things used to be, when markets actually smelled of food. An ethnic market transports the shopper not only to another country but also to another time.

I never know what I'll find in an ethnic market; it's always an adventure and a treasure hunt. Just a few streets from me is a little Japanese market that I had passed without noticing almost daily for two years. There I found the most delicious snack: little dried green peas lightly coated with salt and wasabi (powdered Japanese horseradish) that give just the right kick to the taste buds.

In another direction is an Indian market where I get chick peas and lentils, curry mixtures and tea. An Italian market in another direction sells the best made-on-the-premises Italian sausage I've ever tasted. Near my parents' home in Connecticut is an excellent Greek market that I love to visit. It offers over a dozen kinds of olive oil, big jars of capers in two sizes, a large variety of pastas, tart cherries in glass jars, and tubs of tarama (Greece's answer to caviar.)

garlic and onion powder I never buy onion or garlic salt. It makes no sense to increase the salt in a dish (it's unhealthy) when all you are trying to add is the taste of onion or garlic. Although fresh onion and garlic is wonderful, there are many times when I want a more subtle flavor. I always add onion powder to egg salad, for instance. And garlic powder in salad dressing does not linger on the breath the way its fresh counterpart does.

I like **instant mashed potatoes** (another unfashionable product) not beside the turkey at Thanksgiving (heavens, no) but in homemade bread (preserves moistness,) and to thicken soups and gravies. It also makes the most delicious quickie samosas (Indian turnovers.) Make mashed potatoes with yogurt instead of milk, season with plenty of fried onion, coarsely crushed coriander and mustard seed, and toss in a handful of frozen, thawed baby peas for color. Spread the mixture thinly on big flour tortillas, fold in half and fry on both sides in half butter, half oil. Serve with chutney and yogurt for dunking. Delicious!

mayonnaise While purists may protest, I personally find that making mayonnaise from scratch is not worth the effort. Hellmann's has been my favorite for as long as I can remember. I love the way it tastes, not oily, a bit lemony, not too salty and it's texture is firm enough to hold up in salads.

olive oil is big in fashionable, tony circles, particularly since studies have found that people who come from parts of the world that use it in cooking tend to have healthy hearts. The labeling on olive oils is confusing, however. Although "Extra virgin" designates the first pressing of the olives, oil so labeled can vary in flavor from light and delicate to robust or even rough.

Every market's shelves are loaded with all types and shades, from deep green to almost colorless. Personally, I like a fairly fruity extra-virgin oil for most cooking. When I want less olive flavor, I cut it with a light vegetable oil such as Crisco or Wesson. I try different olive oils all the time because it's fun, but my basic everyday brand is Pompeian. A bit more robust is Goya brand from Spain.

onions I never buy regular-size onions — haven't for years. The big yellow Spanish onions and the large white-skinned variety are the size of a baseball and bigger. They're easier to peel, have a milder, sweeter flavor and — surprise! never cause tears, no matter how much chopping you do. Don't worry that you rarely use so much onion at one time. Just cut off as much as you need and wrap the remainder in plastic. It will keep for over a week in the fridge. The big guys are so much easier to handle and the flavor is so much nicer I'll bet you'll never buy those harsh little devils again.

rice Yes, there are dozens of new rices on the market and they are fun to try. However, for a good, all purpose rice, I think Uncle Ben's long grain white rice (not the "minute" version) can't be beaten. By the way, nutritionally, it's on a par with brown rice.

seasoned salt Lawry's brand is my favorite seasoning for anything roasted (in place of plain salt.) I use it for chicken, turkey, beef, pork, lamb, winter squashes, or root vegetables such as white or sweet potatoes, onions or turnips. Try filling a big pan with a single layer of mixed winter vegetables, dribble with olive oil, sprinkle with Lawry's and lots of rosemary. Bake in a hot oven (425°) until the vegetables are brown at the edges.

sour salt (citric acid) Many people have never used this white granular seasoning. It's the "lemon" in commercial lemon-pepper seasoning. I use it whenever I want to add the tang of lemon without making a dish watery — guacamole is a perfect example. I also reach for it for sauces or dressings. I use it in my lemon cookies because lemon juice changes the crisp texture of my favorite recipe. I also use it on oven-fried chicken because it doesn't make the crust soggy. A traditional ingredient in borscht and stuffed cabbage, you can find it in the Kosher section of your supermarket where it sells out around Passover. It is sold under several labels. Two are Rokeach brand (Newark, NJ) and Emes brand (Lombard, IL) Ben Shapera, third generation in the Emes company says their sour salt comes from Israel where it is made from sugar beets and fruit.

spices I buy small bottles of every different kind of spice I come across. I even have fenugreek (good in curries.) Turmeric, an under-appreciated relative of ginger, is one of my favorites. American cooks use it most mostly in pickling and preserving — chow chows and mustard pickles, that sort of thing. It has many more uses. I make a mix of turmeric, ginger, garlic and minced onion and rub it on meat and chicken before grilling. Or add a generous amount of turmeric plus lots of sliced onions to browned lamb or beef for an exotic North African stew.

An Indian woman from Bombay gave my mother a "never-fail" cough remedy: 1 tablespoon each turmeric and honey dissolved in 1 cup hot milk with a pinch of salt. This remedy can indeed stop a persistent cough in its tracks.

Kept tightly sealed and out of daylight, spices will last a long time. An extensive spice collection is a good investment considering that their cost is pro-rated over years, they take up a tiny bit of space, and they instantly add variety to everyday meals.

tomatoes I never buy any canned tomato product other than whole, peeled tomatoes. Just because they are whole, only the best, perfectly ripened, unbruised tomatoes of the crop can be used for this purpose. When I need tomato sauce, I purée whole canned tomatoes. If I want to get rid of the seeds, I cut each in half and squeeze over a strainer. This is rarely necessary, however. The taste of whole tomatoes that you purée yourself is much fresher than canned tomato sauce.

Winter tomatoes are an abomination. I never touch them. Hard and dry as tennis balls, they are not really ripe because their seductive red color is the result of exposure to gas not sunshine. They will not improve if left on a window sill to ripen. When you need fresh tomatoes out of season, however, there is one salvation. Cherry tomatoes actually do ripen. When fully ripe, they are juicy with a true tomato taste.

vinegar is another staple that has become fashionable. I always have on hand an assortment of vinegars: white vinegar, cider vinegar, red wine vinegar, white wine vinegar, rice wine vinegar, and balsamic vinegar. I usually add extra wine to the wine vinegars — a dose of burgundy for the red, chablis or sherry for the white. I never buy herb flavored vinegar. It's usually more expensive and I prefer to use my own fresh herbs.

Balsamic vinegar is another matter. The real thing has been made in Modeno, Italy for hundreds of years. Traditionally, fermented grape juice is aged in wooden barrels for decades. The resulting *aceto balsamico* is sweet, syrupy, mellow, rare and very expensive. Commercial producers take short cuts to speed up the process but many of these products are quite pleasing in their own right. The best way to find one you like is to try several brands.

A back-door salad & edible flower garden

ONE OF THE LOVELIEST FOOD CUSTOMS to emerge in the last few years has been the use of edible blossoms as garnish and even for eating. Generally these floral embellishments are reserved for fancy, festive occasions like weddings or birthday parties. But why not indulge a bit at other times? I assure you it is so easy to create gaspingly beautiful meals that you will be inclined to scatter blossoms any time spirits, yours or anyone else's, need a lift.

Other cultures are more familiar with the gustatory properties of flowers than we. If you have ever eaten Hot and Sour Soup in a Chinese restaurant, you have undoubtedly eaten lily buds, an ingredient common to most recipes for this popular dish. French pastry chefs today still decorate their richest buttercream creations with candied violets as they did two hundred years ago. Middle Eastern and East Indian markets in the U.S. invariably stock little bottles of rose water for flavoring puddings, breads and pastries. And jasmine tea is popular in the Orient and all over the world.

The best way to assure a ready supply of edible flowers is to plant some. Right outside your kitchen door is a most convenient spot. Grow them side by side with your herbs. The flowers of most herbs are edible and taste just like their leaves. The pale purple flowers of chive, sage or mint are a pretty addition to any salad. Arrange them artfully on top just before serving. In winter when your garden is bare, a few petals from purchased roses can stand in till spring comes.

You will need but a small amount of space for both flowers and herbs. Start as soon as the ground thaws. Planting takes little time once your soil is turned and enriched with compost and fertilizer. Most of the flowers and herbs I recommend here thrive on neglect, endure dry spells, grow vigorously, and tend to crowd out weeds.

One warning: Not all flowers are edible, and some are even poisonous — such as the familiar poinsettia so beloved at Christmastime. Don't experiment by tasting any flower that is unfamiliar to you. Remember the book entitled Please Don't Eat the Daisies? That's good advice for more than purely etiquette reasons; daisies are not on the list of safe edibles.

THIS IS A LIST OF THE PLANTS NOW GROWING IN MY BACK-DOOR SALAD-AND-FLOWER GARDEN.

BASIL is a tender herb that grows best outdoors in the summer. In India basil is believed to be sacred and a protector of the home. The deep purple variety is absolutely gorgeous. Rather than start basil from seed I purchase young plants from a garden shop or supermarket.

BAY is another tender tub plant that can be quite ornamental. I started training mine three years ago from a cutting my father gave me. I removed all but three green, pliable branches growing close together at soil level. When these three were a foot or so tall, I removed all leaves and side growth except for a few sprouts at the top. I then braided the three branches starting from the base and working to the top. Wire twists and a small stake held the branches until they took this shape on their own. This summer, I noticed that the stems were beginning to graft into one trunk and grow bark. The handsome little tree winters at a sunny window in a blue and white Chinese cache pot. When pruning the plant, I dry the leaves to flavor soups and stews.

CHERVIL is a tough perennial with feathery foliage that tastes like anise. It is lovely sprinkled over cold salmon instead of dill or in shrimp or crab salad. It is invasive and must be regularly weeded out of its neighbors' space.

CILANTRO is an herb you either love or hate. I hated it the first time I tasted it. Now it's one herb I am never without. I grow it outside in the summer and buy it fresh at the market in the winter. The flavor is lost in drying.

CICORIA, also known as Italian Dandelions, Radichetti and Asparagus Chicory has become one of my favorite salad greens. The seeds (available from Hart Seeds, Wethersfield, CT 06109) are sown in the early spring. Unlike lettuce, these greens do not "bolt" in hot weather and the plants continue to make tender new leaves all summer and well past fall frosts. In late summer, sprays of pale blue aster-like flowers appear in the morning and fade by noon. (No, despite the name "dandelion," the flowers are not the familiar lawn variety yellow pin cushions.) The flavor is pleasantly pungent. Wild dandelions, the kind found in the lawn, are also edible.

DAYLILIES (hemerocallis) come in many colors and shapes — even ruffled or double, in shades from pale butter yellow to lavender to deep, rich red. The wild orange variety blooms in June; most cultivated ones begin blooming a bit later. Order from nursery catalogs or look for different colors in garden shops. With planning you can have one or another daylily blooming continuously for months. All daylily flowers are edible.

DILL is easy to grow and especially useful if you like pickled vegetables. Try covering zucchini spears with a mixture of white vinegar and water, half-and-half, heated to boiling. Add slices of onion, sprigs of dill and 1 teaspoon of salt per big jar. Leave in refrigerator overnight.

HORSERADISH is easy to grow. The young leaves taste like the horseradish root but milder. Finely shredded young horseradish leaves are a tasty addition to any salad that needs a bit of zing. The tough thick roots are available in the grocery store in fall or winter. Peel and grind slices with salt and vinegar in a food processor. Then plant a few pieces in the ground, if it isn't already frozen, and you will see growth in the spring.

JOHNNY JUMP UPS (a.k.a. violas) are tiny purple flowers that resemble a cross between violets and pansies. They are edible. They don't bloom as long as pansies unless you faithfully remove the spent flower heads — a chore that I mostly forego.

JERUSALEM ARTICHOKE (a.k.a. sunchokes) is a relative of the sunflower as its blossom, which appears late in the season, suggests. After the first hard frost, harvest the tubers. They taste like artichoke bottoms. This 7-foot tall plant is vigorous and tends to take over its neighbors' space. I started mine from a couple of tubers I bought in the grocery store. The cut flowers make beautiful bouquets.

LEMON THYME A small pot of this pretty tiny-leafed shrub purchased years ago has spread in my garden to the point that it needs to be cut back severely every spring. Delicate white flowers appear throughout the summer. Use sprigs of the flowers as garnish on chicken and fish dishes. Harvest young sprigs throughout the growing season and dry up-side-down in bunches for a year-round supply.

MARIGOLD is an easy-to-grow hardy annual. Its bright golden, edible flower with a peppery flavor looks beautiful in salads. Or use the flowers to decorate a lemon cake or bowls of strawberries and blueberries. A famous chicken purveyor once bragged that his chickens got their beautiful yellow skin from the marigold petals in their feed.

MINT, a perennial, comes in many varieties. There's spearmint and peppermint, of course, but there's also curly mint, orange mint, pineapple mint, variegated mint and a little creeping gound cover mint that grows between stepping stones in milder climes. I dry mint for using in Greek salads in the winter or for mint tea.

MUSTARD GREENS have pretty yellow edible mustard-flavored flowers. The young leaves are pungent and very good in salads. The plants often self-sow.

NASTURTIUMS, those gaudy show-offs, come in dwarf and tall forms with yellow, red, hot pink and orange flowers and even with green and white variegated leaves. Both flowers and leaves are edible. Sow directly in the spot where plants are to grow. To speed germination, I soak the caper-sized seeds in water overnight. Nasturtiums bloom continuously right up until frost. The seeds can be pickled and used like capers.

OREGANO is a tough perennial that will crowd out weeds and return year after year. Fresh oregano is intensely aromatic.

PANSIES are another of my favorites; I love their cranky faces. They are a big payoff for very little money or work. Buy flats of your favorite colors (a big grouping of all the same color is more effective than many colors) and set the plants into borders after the last frost. They will reward you with continuous blooms for the entire summer.

PARSLEY is a biennial, meaning that it lives for two years. It is often self-sowing but you can easily replant it in the early spring. If you forget, buy a potted parsley plant in the grocery store, remove the pot and pop the plant in the ground. I prefer the flat-leaf Italian parsley.

RHUBARB is not an herb and its flower is certainly not edible. In fact, its leaves are poisonous. However, the tender pink stalks of spring make the most delicious strawberry-rhubarb jam. Because rhubarb is high in pectin, you never need to add commercial pectin to get the jam to "set up." Use equal amounts of fruit and sugar. That's all there is to it.

"RHUBARB" CHARD is another easy-to-grow, ornamental salad vegetable. It is not related to rhubarb, but has similar red stems. Although chard is often served cooked in the same way as spinach, I like to use the young tender leaves raw in salads. The bright red stems are a pleasant surprise and the spinach-y flavor is a nice change from blander greens.

ROSES, the queen of flowers, are edible. Isn't that incredible. Whole buds are too beautiful to eat; however, coral or pink petals tossed among tender green shoots of lettuce are just the right touch. Since my first criterion for choosing plants is, "Does it thrive on neglect?" I avoided roses for years believing them to be too demanding and fussy to accept my casual gardening style. I now know better. Other than deep mulching in the winter, regular fertilizing and a dusting with fungicide during humid spells, roses need little care. Even as far north as Massachusetts, I have picked the "last rose of summer" on Thanksgiving Day.

SAGE is a tough perennial with handsome gray leaves and tiny purple flowers. Both flowers and stems make beautiful garnishes. At Thanksgiving, I fry sprigs of fresh sage in hot oil until crisp and use as a garnish around the turkey. The flavor is just wonderful.

SQUASH BLOSSOMS are edible. I think the most elegant thing to do with them is to pick them just before they open, dip them in a light batter and fry them until crisp and golden. Sprinkle them with coarse salt just before serving. A magical first course. The lightest crust is made from equal parts of rice flour, cornstarch and flour with just enough water to make the mixture the consistency of pancake batter (no egg.)

TARRAGON and **ROSEMARY** are tender perennials. I grow them in tubs outside over the summer then winter them in a cool basement near a sunny window. Rosemary can be trained into all sorts of decorative shapes. I've seen plants trimmed in a conical shape to resemble a Christmas tree, grown on one tall trunk with a pom-pom of foliage at the top, or trained on a wire form in a ball shape. Rosemary often has difficulty surviving the transition to indoors because it is prone to attacks of fungus and mildew, both on the leaves and in the soil. Allow the soil to dry thoroughly between waterings. Never allow the pot to stand in water. To retard mildew on the leaves, mist with a mixture of 1 teaspoon of baking powder dissolved in 1 quart of water.

antipasto
nibblers' heaven

How MANY NIBBLERS DO YOU KNOW? I mean, people who always want just a taste of this-or-that until, innumerable tastings later, they have consumed the equivalent of a huge meal. In truth, everybody is a potential nibbler because it's such a fun way to eat.

Antipasto is what Italians call the dish that comes before the pasta, or the first course. Sometimes an antipasto will be one or two, usually cold but sometimes hot, savories. In this country, Italian restaurants often offer big, brimming platters containing a dozen of their most delectable specialties. Antipasti are designed in heaven for nibblers. After polishing off a plate of them, however, diners often find that they have no room left for the main course. This being the case, why not make a dinner of the antipasto and then go right to dessert, espresso and Sambuca?

There's no end to the dishes that can appear on *your* antipasto table. Many will require no preparation — you simply select them from the deli counter or open a jar or can. The homemade items can be fast and easy, relying primarily on what is fresh and appealing at the produce counter. Even four or five simple dishes will not put a strain on your time or energy.

If you live near a good little Italian market, that's the place to find the best selection: cold cuts, olives, jars of peppers — sweet and hot — garlicky artichokes in oil, tins of sardines and anchovies and imported cheeses. Ask for advice and samples from the cold case if something is unfamiliar to you. Your local supermarket may carry many good products, too. Again, ask for a taste.

By the way, have you ever walked into a really good Italian restaurant and said to yourself, My, this place smells great! I wish my kitchen would smell like this when I cook Italian. Here's the secret: Great Italian cooking is basically simple foods made with the best ingredients. When shopping for ingredients, it's always worth paying extra for the best.

HOW TO DO AN ANTIPASTO PLATTER   Your platter may include any number of ready-to-serve items: one or more varieties of meats such as salami, prosciutto (salted, dried ham), bresaola (salted, dried beef), mortadella (a delicate baloney-like sausage dotted with peppercorns, coriander seeds, or pistachios); and cheeses such as fontina, gorgonzola, fresh mozzarella, and provolone. Also look for boxes of long, skinny bread sticks and loaves of coarse Italian bread or focaccia, a flat loaf topped with olive oil, rosemary, and onions or garlic. Whether you prepare individual plates or one high, wide and handsome platter, begin with a bed of ruffled lettuce leaves. Bread sticks can be wrapped with salami or served as dippers for bean paté. All dishes can be prepared hours or a day or two in advance. Here are some antipasti to get you going.

antipasti asparagus with walnuts

Cook asparagus just until bright green and tender-crisp. Dress with oil and lemon juice and sprinkle with chopped toasted walnuts and coarse salt.

broccoli with pine nuts & capers

Parboil broccoli until tender-crisp. Heat a handful of pine nuts and a clove of garlic cut in quarters in a little olive oil until nuts are lightly browned. Remove garlic pieces and pour oil over broccoli. Just before serving squeeze lemon over, sprinkle with capers and salt to taste.

italian tuna salad

Canned tuna in oil is only as good as the oil it's packed in. I like to buy tuna packed in water and add my own fruity oil.

Drain a can of water-packed tuna and mash lightly with a fork. Sprinkle with olive oil and add thinly sliced carrots, minced onion, chopped green olives with pimiento and minced parsley. Chill.

stuffed artichokes

Simmer artichokes (stems trimmed and leaf tips snipped) in salted water until a leaf pulls off easily. Drain and cool. Using a heavy knife, quarter artichokes then scoop out choke and small leaves. Fill hollow with a mixture of breadcrumbs, garlic, olive oil or melted butter, minced parsley and Parmesan or Asiago cheese and bake in a 400° oven for 20 minutes or until browned. Serve hot or cold with lemon wedges.

stuffed mushrooms

Fill mushroom caps with above filling to which you have added the minced mushroom stems plus a bit of oregano or marjoram and grated provolone in place of Parmesan. Bake in a 400° oven for 20 minutes or until browned on top.

stuffed eggs

Halve hard-boiled eggs and remove the yolks. Mash yolks with mayonnaise, finely minced scallions, anchovy paste and crushed capers and pile into whites. Decorate tops with a leaf of parsley and a few whole capers.

preserving beautiful color

Prolonged marinating in an acidic dressing will cause broccoli and many other green vegetables to lose their bright color. Always add acidic ingredients to green vegetables just before serving. Red vegetables like red peppers or purple cabbage are not adversely affected.

antipasti

cannelini spread

2   cups (1 can) cannelini beans, drained
1/4   cup olive oil
1   tablespoon *each* wine vinegar and
       lemon juice
1   tablespoon *each* minced scallion
       and parsley
       a pinch of crumbled rosemary
       black pepper

Mash beans lightly and add remaining ingredients.
Chill. Serve with bread or bread sticks for dunking.

cooked zucchini salad

*Believe it or not, many vegetable-averse kids will eat
zucchini prepared this way.*

Cut zucchini into thin slices. Heat a little olive oil
in large skillet and add a clove or two of garlic. Brown
lightly then add zucchini and stir fry until crisp-tender.
In small jar mix one part vinegar with 2 parts olive oil.
Add to zucchini in pan and heat through. Do not allow
zucchini to become soft. Add a generous grind of pepper
and salt to taste. Serve hot or chilled.

fennel & orange salad

*The licorice flavor and crunch of fennel combines
beautifully with the tang of oranges. Use about equal
amounts of each.*

Slice fennel vertically into thin sticks. Grate a
little rind from an orange, then peel and slice desired
number of oranges into segments. Combine with fennel,
add grated peel and sprinkle with fruity olive oil, lemon
juice, salt and a generous grating of black pepper.
Garnish with wisps of fennel leaves. Chill.

spanzanella

(Italian Bread Salad)

This is one of my favorite ways to use the good garden tomatoes of summer. Coarse, crusty bread and juicy, very ripe tomatoes are the secret.

6 to 8	cups day-old French or Italian bread, cut in 1-inch cubes
1/2	cup *each* diced red onion and diced seeded cucumber
3	large very ripe tomatoes or 1 box cherry tomatoes, coarsely chopped
1/2	cup minced parsley
1/4	cup minced fresh basil
1/4	cup balsamic vinegar or wine vinegar
1/2	cup olive oil
	generous grating of coarsely ground black pepper, salt to taste

Toss all ingredients together and chill.

baked potato salad

This one is different. Not a trace of mayonnaise, celery or onion but one of the best potato salads I've ever tasted. Why is this so good? It's just one of those magical combinations that is much more than the sum of its parts.

Bake small red skin potatoes in a 400° oven until skins begin to brown and potatoes are squeezably soft (35-40 minutes.) Cool and slice into chunks. In small jar mix one part vinegar, 2 parts olive oil and garlic, freshly ground black pepper and salt to taste. Pour over potatoes. Add chopped sun dried tomatoes, a generous amount of minced flat-leaf parsley and sliced Mediterranean-style olives. Chill.

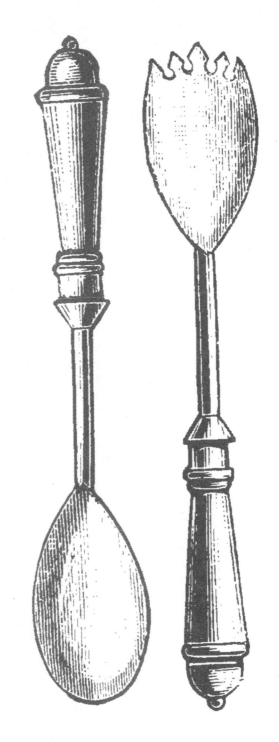

antipasti

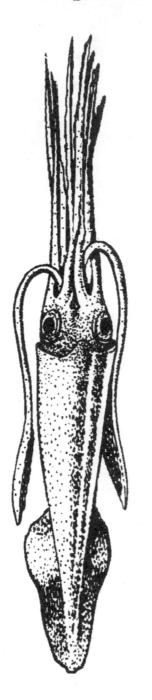

insalata di calamari

If the word squid makes you think of rubber bands, you've had overcooked squid. An Italian chef taught me this sure-fire secret for tender squid: no more than two minutes in a large pot of boiling water. Blanching the onion with the squid takes away the onion's harshness.

1	pound squid, cleaned
1/3	cup olive oil
1	small onion, thinly sliced vertically
3/4	cup inner stalks and leaves of celery, sliced thin
2	tablespoons lemon juice
2	tablespoons white wine vinegar
1/4	cup white wine
1/4	cup *each* chopped parsley and basil
1/2	teaspoon thyme
1	small clove garlic, mashed
	salt, black pepper, red pepper flakes to taste

Cut cleaned squid bodies into rings, leave tentacles whole. Drop squid and chopped onion into a large stock pot of boiling water. Immediately turn off heat, cover pot and let stand just 2 minutes. Drain into colander. Add remaining ingredients to squid and onion and chill thoroughly.

Italians love their calamari (squid), however, many people are leery of eating squid, fearing that it will be fishy or rubbery. Neither is the case when squid is prepared properly. In fact, squid has a delicate flavor and texture that surprises people trying it for the first time.

Years ago when I was a novice cook I was standing at the fish counter waiting to be served and I happened to strike up a conversation with an Italian woman standing next to me. She mentioned that she was buying squid (her favorite seafood, she said) for dinner that night. I asked her to tell me how to use this odd and intriguing creature. She gave me detailed instructions on how to clean them and a recipe for spaghetti sauce with stuffed squid.

I decided to try her recipe that night. My children were both in grade school at the time and they and their friends took quite an interest in watching me pull the innards out of the squids' tubular bodies and cut the tentacles from their heads. I stuffed the bodies with bread crumbs, garlic, olive oil and oregano and sauteed them in olive oil along with the tentacles. The squid were then added to a basic marinara sauce. Since I, like every other parent, was intimately familiar with my children's expansive list of inedible "yukky" foods, I didn't even bother to ask them if they would like to try Spaghetti with Squid Sauce.

The sauce simmered for an hour while the kids went out to play. They returned promptly at the time I had said the meal would be done. With not a moment's hesitation, they scooped sauce onto their spaghetti, squabbling over who was getting the most tentacles. Ten minutes later their plates were clean and I was shaking my head in astonishment.

about squid

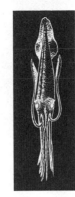

how to clean squid

1   Pull the head and the insides from the body.

2   Under running water, peel the purplish, speckled skin from the body and the fins.

3   Reach your finger inside the tubular body and pull out the thin, cellophane-like "spine."

4   Squeeze out the rest of the innards and rinse the body well.

5   Cut the tentacles in front of the eyes and pull out the hard little beak at the center of the tentacles.

6   Cut the body into whatever shape you prefer. You may cut it into rings or slit the tube, lay the squid flat and cut strips.

antipasti

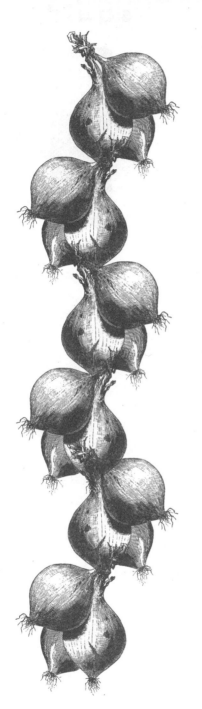

caponata

This dish is Italy's answer to France's ratatouille. It's a marvelous way to use up the excesses of a home garden. This version is the best ever. Two secrets: Unpeeled lemon slices add a special flavor as they cook along with the vegetables; and the vegetables should be cooked briefly to retain just a bit of crispness.

1/2	cup olive oil
1	large onion, thinly sliced vertically
1	stalk celery, thinly sliced on the diagonal
1	medium eggplant, unpeeled, cubed
2	medium zucchinis, sliced on diagonal
1 1/2	cups canned whole tomatoes, cut in chunks
1	teaspoon dry basil or several sprigs of fresh
2	cloves garlic, crushed
1/3	cup each capers and parsley
1/2	cup Mediterranean-style olives, pitted
1	lemon, thinly sliced
	salt and pepper to taste

Heat oil and cook onion until wilted. Add celery, eggplant, zucchini and garlic and continue cooking stirring frequently. When vegetables begin to soften, add tomatoes, lemon slices, basil, capers, parsley, and olives and simmer for 10 minutes or until vegetables are tender. Season with salt and coarse black pepper. Chill overnight.

italian chopped salad

Crunchy and delicious as well as colorful.

Cut approximately equal parts of the following vegetables into a 1/4-inch dice: carrots, peppers (any combination of red, yellow, orange, purple or green), celery, fennel, tomato, and green onion. Cut one or two 1/4-inch thick slices of mortadella and an equal amount of provolone cheese into 1/4-inch cubes. Combine all. Dress with oil and vinegar to moisten, season with salt and pepper and chill well.

cold linguini alla putanesca

This is a cold variation of the classic "Whore's-style" spaghetti sauce said to be what Italian prostitutes whipped up for their favorite customers from ingredients they happened to have on hand — tomatoes, olives, capers and anchovies. This version is based on canned tomatoes but you can use fresh when they are in season.

12	ounces linguini, broken into short pieces, cooked and drained
1	can peeled whole tomatoes, drained (reserve juice for another use)
1	clove garlic, mashed
1/4	cup fruity olive oil
2	tablespoons capers
1/3	cup pitted, sliced Mediterranean-style olives
3	tablespoons finely minced anchovies
1/4	cup minced flat leaf parsley
1/2	teaspoon dry oregano
1/4	cup fresh basil, chopped, or 1 tablespoon dried
	a generous grating of black pepper and salt to taste

Garnish: Parmesan or Romano cheese, olives, parsley

Roughly chop tomatoes in food processor. Pour over cooked pasta and add remaining ingredients. Chill well to meld flavors.

PRESENTATION Pile pasta on plates and garnish with olives and long sprigs of parsley. On top, with a vegetable peeler scrape large flakes of Parmesan or Romano cheese.

caesar salad

SERVES FOUR

Never waste a grand opportunity: Caesar Salad is food as theater. Don't make it in the kitchen and bring it to the table already assembled. A restaurateur in Acapulco created this famous salad back in the early Twenties. The original version was prepared with great pomp and ceremony by the waiter at the table in view of admiring diners. It's not a bit difficult but if you are having guests, have a dress rehearsal so you can perform from memory. As you add each ingredient don't skimp on the flourishes. In other words, ham it up!

You'll need a big wooden salad bowl and a handsome tray to hold the ingredients. Use your best-looking salt shaker, fresh bottles of mustard and Worcestershire sauce and attractive small dishes to hold other ingredients. Most important: use the smaller inner leaves of the lettuce and leave them whole. This salad is traditionally eaten with the fingers. Much more dramatic!

Arrange on your tray in the following order

	a salt shaker
1	clove peeled garlic, in a garlic press
5	chopped anchovies on a small dish
	a jar of Dijon mustard and a small spoon
	a bottle of Worcestershire sauce
1/3	cup olive oil, measured into a cruet or bowl
1	lemon cut in half, seeds removed
1	coddled egg (boiled 1 minute) and a knife for cracking it
3-4	heads of romaine lettuce, just the inner light green leaves, left whole, washed, spun dry, chilled on a platter
1/4	cup Parmesan cheese, freshly grated, in a small bowl
1	generous cup croutons (homemade from good French or Italian bread, browned in olive oil with a bit of garlic added toward the end)
	a pepper grinder
	a small clean dish towel for wiping your hands if necessary

Hail,

PRESENTATION   Have a large wooden salad bowl with serving pieces, chilled dinner plates and your tray of ingredients ready at the table. As your guests watch, lightly sprinkle the salad bowl with salt. Squeeze the garlic into the bottom of the bowl and rub it into the salt using the back of your salad spoon. Add chopped anchovies and continue rubbing until a paste is formed. Add a teaspoon of mustard. With your knife whack the egg in half and empty the shells into the bowl. Stir vigorously into garlic mixture. When blended, add three shakes of Worcestershire and stir again. Dribble in the olive oil while continuing to stir vigorously. Add the lettuce leaves all at once and roll gently in the oil mixture to coat. Squeeze the lemon halves over lettuce and roll again. With a final flourish grind a few twists of pepper over the salad, sprinkle with Parmesan, add croutons and give the salad one last toss. Bow to thunderous applause and serve.

VARIATION
Spinach Caesar — Use whole spinach leaves in place of romaine.

Caesar!

blistered peppers
with mozzarella

This dish is unusual in that you don't remove the skin of the peppers. The charred skin adds to the taste and appearance. I don't know why most recipes tell you to go through the time-consuming job of removing it.

Visuals are everything! This is a beautiful (but so easy) "composed" salad. The colors are nothing short of riotous: green, red, yellow, orange, purple, white, and black. Use dinner plates, not cramped little salad plates, and decorate a bigger "canvas."

If you've never tasted fresh mozzarella, you are in for a pleasant surprise. Most of us are familiar only with those prepackaged rubber balls found in the dairy case. The fresh variety can be located in Italian groceries and occasionally in upscale supermarkets. The creamy globes are generally displayed immersed in water in the deli case. Fresh mozzarella is perishable and must be used within a few days. Do not substitute the packaged variety unless you will be using it in a cooked dish. When a recipes calls for using it uncooked, as here, it's better to use a different cheese of top quality.

8	bell peppers, red, green, yellow, and orange, if possible, sliced vertically into strips
1	large onion, sliced vertically
1/4	cup fruity olive oil
2	cloves garlic, minced
1	teaspoon oregano
	coarse salt and fresh ground pepper to taste

Spread sliced peppers and onions on sheets in one layer, keeping colors together. Sprinkle with oil and minced garlic. Broil peppers as close to heat source as possible, turning occasionally until peppers have black blisters all over them (about 20 minutes). Cool and season with salt, pepper and oregano.

3 or 4 balls fresh mozzarella (3/4 to 1 pound), cubed, or another mild, semi-soft cheese like Fontina, Muenster or Havarti

Calamata olives

tomatoes

lemon wedges

assorted salad greens

PRESENTATION Arrange greens on plates. Top with broiled peppers and onions and cubes of cheese. Garnish with olives, tomatoes, lemon wedges. Pass cruets of fruity olive oil and balsamic vinegar, coarse salt and a pepper mill.

Serve with crusty loaves of Italian bread split, lightly spread with olive, oil, garlic and rosemary and heated piping hot. For dessert try pears poached in sweet Marsala wine garnished with a few slivers of lemon peel and a puff of whipped cream, if desired.

italian sub salad

SERVES FOUR

This colorful, crunchy salad contains all the ingredients of a good Italian submarine sandwich, plus a couple of extras. Layer it in a trifle bowl for maximum visual impact.

salami & cheese medley

Cut into 1/3-inch dice and combine the following:

1/2	pound hard salami or pepperoni
2	balls fresh mozzarella
1/3	pound provolone or fontina cheese
1	bulb fennel
1	small zucchini and/or yellow summer squash
1	red bell pepper
2	cups stale sub rolls, cut into 1/2 inch cubes
3	cups chopped ripe tomatoes tossed with a handful of chopped fresh basil (or 1 tablespoon dry)
1	1-pound can canellini beans, rinsed and drained
1	small head romaine lettuce, shredded

Garnish: olives, capers, anchovies

Put a layer of bread cubes in bottom of glass salad bowl. Add a layer of tomatoes, then beans, then the salami medley. Continue layering in that order until the ingredients are used up. Pour dressing over and refrigerate several hours. Just before serving, sprinkle top of salad with a generous amount of chopped Italian flat parsley, olives, capers and anchovies.

italian dressing

Whisk together:

1/3	cup red wine vinegar
2	tablespoons lemon juice
2	cloves garlic, crushed
1	teaspoon *each* dry mustard and sugar
1 1/4	cups fruity olive oil
1/2	teaspoon dry oregano or marjoram
	salt and pepper

PRESENTATION Allow guests to help themselves from the bowl. Serve with Polenta Gnocchi (see Go-Withs.)

chicken & rice *with* sour cream & grapes

This elegant salad is a complete meal in itself. The unusual combination of flavors and textures gives it a subtle sophistication. I have made this for vegetarians with just rice and no chicken and it does not suffer from the omission. I have also made it with all chicken and no rice. If you have a mixed group of vegetarians and omnivores, make portions of rice alone and rice with chicken. Adding the toasted almonds at the last minute preserves their crunchiness.

3/4	cup raw rice, cooked according to package directions
1 1/2	cups cooked chicken breast, diced
2/3	cup coarsely chopped salted cashews
1	cup seedless grapes, halved

Garnish: small bunches of grapes, lettuce leaves, salted cashews

Combine chicken, rice and grapes with dressing and chill 1 hour to blend flavors.

creamy tarragon dressing

1/2	cup "lite" sour cream
	juice of 1 lime
1/4	cup *each* mayonnaise and tarragon vinegar
1	tablespoon fresh tarragon, minced, or 1 teaspoon dried
1/4	cup *each* minced parsley and chives
1/4	teaspoon white pepper
	salt to taste

PRESENTATION   Reserve some chopped cashews for garnish and fold in the remainder just before serving. Line plates with lettuce and pile on chicken rice mixture. Sprinkle nuts over top. Arrange grape clusters along side. Serve with hot Blueberry or Cranberry Muffins. (see Go-Withs.)

poached salmon *with* diced aspic

SERVES FOUR

Nothing is more elegant than cold poached salmon. Allow a half pound salmon per person and be very careful not to overcook it. I love to serve this on the Fourth of July with strawberry-blueberry shortcake for dessert.

| 2 | pounds salmon fillets, from thick end |

poaching broth
Combine and bring to a boil:

4	cups water
1/2	cup dry white wine
4	cups bouillon (Knorr makes vegetable and fish cubes but chicken cubes work equally well)
1	slice onion, chopped a handful of celery leaves
1/2	lemon, peel on, sliced

| 2/3 | cup frozen, tiny green peas |
| 2 | carrots sliced paper thin or julienned |

Garnish: mayonnaise, lemon, dill, cucumber, chives, watercress

Remove all hidden bones. To do this, with your fingers find and pull out the line of bones that runs along one side of the fillet. There will be one bone at each of the white striations in the pink flesh.

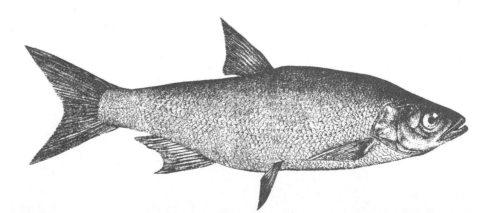

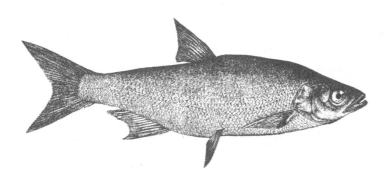

Gently simmer the fish in the broth, covered, for about 15-20 minutes or until it is opaque. Don't wait for it to become "flaky" or it will be overdone. Remove the fish with a wide spatula and chill. Strain stock through a mesh sieve leaving solids in pan. If you see a film of oil on top of the stock, remove it by placing a paper towel flat on the surface and quickly pulling it off. Return broth to rinsed pan and correct seasoning. Add peas and carrots and simmer for 3 minutes. Remove with a slotted spoon. Soften 2 packages plain gelatin in 1/4 cup water and add to 4 cups of hot fish stock. Stir to dissolve. Pour into a shallow pan to a depth of about 1/3 inch and refrigerate to set.

PRESENTATION   When fish has chilled, carefully peel off skin and center fillets on large chilled platter. Run a knife criss-cross through congealed aspic to cut it into a 1/3 inch dice. Lift aspic with a spatula and arrange with peas and carrots on both sides of fish. Mix about a cup of mayonnaise with lemon juice to taste and pour in a strip down center of fish. Sprinkle with finely minced chives, dill or cucumber and decorate ends of platter with watercress and lemon wedges. Serve with Potatoes Caroline (see Go-Withs) and corn on the cob.

paté platter

This is one of those buysum-makesum dishes that combine store-bought foods with additions you make yourself. Many supermarkets now carry delicious meat patés in their cheese section or deli case. Since paté is so rich, I always feel guilty eating it as an appetizer and then piling a dinner on top. On the other hand, I hate the thought of giving up paté all together. The compromise: Paté for dinner! Buy one or two good meat patés and serve with these two easy additions you make yourself: beautiful golden carrot paté and diced emerald aspic. Add a crusty loaf of bread, a robust wine, and indulge!

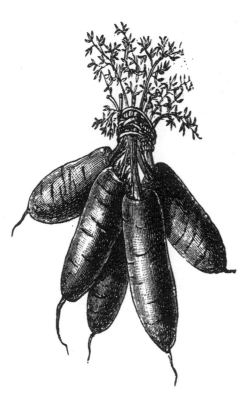

carrot paté

1 1/2 pounds carrots, cut in 2-inch lengths

3	eggs
1/2	cup mayonnaise
2	tablespoons wine vinegar
1/2	teaspoon thyme
1/2	teaspoon salt
	dash hot sauce
1 1/2	tablespoons grated onion

Cook carrots in water to cover for 10 minutes. Drain, well. Add remaining ingredients to bowl of processor and puree thoroughly. Pour into a greased 9x5-inch loaf pan and bake 35 to 40 minutes or until center tests done. Cool 10 minutes and invert on a plate. Chill and serve in slices dressed with a dab of mayonnaise and a few capers.

emerald aspic

1 1/2 cups chicken bouillon

1/2 cup dry white wine

1 tablespoon lemon juice

1 envelope unflavored gelatin

1 cup watercress leaves

Add gelatin to wine and allow to soften. Heat wine mixture with bouillon stirring until gelatin is thoroughly melted. Add lemon juice and cool to room temperature. Purée aspic with watercress then pour into shallow pan and refrigerate until set. Cut into small dice.

peppercorn vinaigrette

1/3 cup wine vinegar

2/3 cup olive oil

1 tablespoon hot water

1/2 teaspoon salt

1 teaspoon black peppercorns

Purée all in processor until pepper is coarsely cracked.

PRESENTATION   Line plates with a mound of pale-colored greens such as endive or hearts of Bibb lettuce. Place slices of meat and carrot paté alongside greens and surround with diced aspic, cornichons or other small pickles, or pickled cocktail onions. Serve peppercorn vinaigrette on side for dressing greens. Pass warm loaves of the crustiest, chewiest bread you can find and sweet butter.

chinese chicken salad

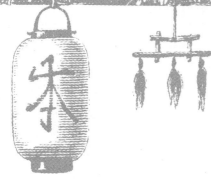

Years ago an associate and I attended a buffet banquet sponsored by The Women's Culinary Guild of Boston. We strolled among a score of tables and sampled dozens of fabulous, elegant dishes. But one dish in particular stopped us in our tracks. The label identified it as Chinese Chicken Salad, a humble enough name, but we spent a good half hour examining a plateful trying to figure out what made it so darn delicious. It was succulent and crunchy and gorgeous with a white cloud of crispy noodles surrounding juicy, sesame-crusted chicken morsels. To this day I rate it as one of the best chicken dishes I have ever put in my mouth. Over the years I've come across numerous recipes for Chinese Chicken Salad (an American creation as it turns out) but never the version that first stole my heart. It took quite a bit of experimenting before I reproduced it. Here it is. This version involves several steps to fry the chicken, noodles and won tons but it's well worth the effort.

2	ounces cellophane noodles
1/2	cup peanut oil
10	won ton wrappers, quartered

Fry noodles in small batches in hot oil just until puffed. Drain on paper towels. In same oil, fry won ton wrappers a few at a time until golden. Drain on paper towels. Reserve the oil.

1	pound skinless, boneless chicken breasts
1/3	cup hoisin sauce
2/3	cup sesame seeds

Marinate chicken in hoisin sauce for one hour. Drain, roll in sesame seeds and quickly sauté in reserved oil until golden. Drain and chill.

1	large firm head of iceberg lettuce
1	small bunch scallions, thinly sliced on the diagonal
1	bunch flat parsley, chopped
1	bunch cilantro, chopped

Soak whole head of lettuce in ice water for 15 minutes. Drain and chill for 1 hour. Slice whole head into 1 inch cubes. Do not separate leaves.

ginger dressing

Combine in a jar:

1	teaspoon grated fresh ginger
1/4	cup light soy sauce
2	teaspoons sugar
2	tablespoons rice wine or dry sherry
2	tablespoons vinegar
1	tablespoon dark sesame oil
1/3	cup peanut oil

Cellophane noodles, hoisin sauce, and won ton wrappers are available in the Chinese foods section of many supermarkets and all Asian markets.

PRESENTATION At meal time gently toss lettuce cubes, parsley, cilantro and scallions with dressing. Distribute evenly over a large platter. Pile chicken pieces in center, adding any accumulated juices, surround with cellophane noodles and tuck fried wonton quarters around chicken.

a *Taste of h*EAVEN

THAI

THE FIRST TIME I TASTED THAI FOOD, I thought this must be what food is like in heaven. It was in a little hole-in-the-wall restaurant in a seedy, down-at-the-heels section of town. At any hour of any day, the restaurant was always crowded. This just goes to show that the old adage about the three secrets of business success being "Location, location and location" is not true for restaurants. The secret of success is "Taste, taste, taste!"

Thai cooks reach for a bottle of their ubiquitous fish sauce as automatically as we reach for salt and pepper. Fish sauce is a briny fermented distillate something like liquid anchovies. Its odor and taste are strong and fishy. Fear not! When a small amount is added to the most delicate dishes its own flavor virtually disappears. Fish sauce can be found in most Asian markets.

Many Westerners recoil at the mere name "fish sauce." But other cuisines employ similar fishy flavorings. In Mediterranean countries, anchovies enhance the flavor of meat and vegetable classics, from spaghetti sauce to pork roasts. Many Chinese meat and vegetable dishes are flavored with oyster sauce, dried tiny shrimp or other dried creatures of the sea. And our old stand-by Worcestershire sauce contains, among other things — anchovies and/or sardines.

So you see fish sauce is not at all unfamiliar in even the tamest American kitchen where it serves to enhance and blend other distinctive flavors.

This strange phenomenon, by the way, also occurs in perfume formulations. Perfumers add to floral blends tiny amounts of animal scents like civit and musk that alone would smell offensive. These pungent substances round out and tone down florals that otherwise would come across as cloyingly sweet.

random thoughts on cooking in Thai

- Thai seasonings vary considerably in strength. When trying fish sauce or any other flavoring for the first time, use sparingly until you get a sense of its potency.

- Don't make the mistake of purchasing coconut cream rather than coconut milk for Thai dishes. The first is a sweetened concoction often found in the bar supply section of your market. It is used for many mixed drinks, perhaps the most famous of which is the piña colada. Coconut milk is not sweetened and tastes just like liquefied fresh coconut. Thai chefs use it in sauces the way French chefs use cream.

- Thai chefs would no more send a dish to the table without a garnish than our chefs would omit salt. Often it's simply slices of fruit or a sprinkling of chopped cilantro or peanuts.

- The most important secret of Thai or any other Asian cooking is to chop and measure everything before you heat the pan. If you have to mince a piece of ginger or soak a dry mushroom during the cooking process, you run the risk of overcooking whatever you have going in the pan. Nothing ruins a lovely Chinese or Thai dish quicker than over-cooked meats or soft vegetables.

Mint is the most wonderful herb: once planted in the ground it asks nothing from us. Even if you have a postage stamp yard you can tuck mint into any sunny spot, add water and then totally ignore it and it will reward you by returning and flourishing season after season. Fresh mint is a worthwhile addition to many Thai and Middle Eastern salads. Ask a friend who has a plant to dig you a clump or you can purchase spearmint, peppermint or even green and yellow variegated pineapple mint at a garden store.

random thoughts on cooking in Thai (continued)

- The best test for doneness in green vegetables is their color. As soon as vegetables such as beans, broccoli or spinach turn bright green, they are done or almost done. Another minute or two is usually all that is required.

- Lemon grass is expensive, hard to find, perishable, and not always easy to work with. Grated lemon rind is an excellent substitute. Grated lime peel is a good substitute for kaffir lime leaves, a common ingredient in Thai cooking that's equally difficult to find. Both are a much better trade than parsley is for cilantro.

- The easiest way to prepare ginger is to cut a piece from one end of the tuber, peel about half an inch, and grate it on an old-fashioned box grater.

thai steak salad
(front cover)

SERVES SIX

1 1/2	pounds beef steak (flank works well, a whole tenderloin for a grand occasion) rubbed with soy sauce and peanut oil
1	head red leaf or other tender lettuce, leaves cut in half lengthwise
1	small red onion, thinly sliced vertically
2	scallions, thinly sliced diagonally
2	heads Belgian endive, thinly sliced lengthwise

mint dressing

In small jar combine:

1 or 2	cloves of garlic, chopped
4	jalapeño peppers, preferably fresh but bottled will do, sliced thin
1 to 2	tablespoon fish sauce
2	tablespoons soy sauce
	grated rind of 1/2 lime
1/2	cup lime juice (4 to 5 limes)
1	tablespoon sugar
3	tablespoons chopped cilantro
1/4	cup chopped fresh mint, or 3 tablespoons dry mint
1/4	cup peanut oil

Prepare dressing and set aside. Prepare vegetables. Grill or broil steak to the desired degree of doneness. Cool to room temperature.

PRESENTATION Lay sliced lettuce leaves lengthwise on plates and top with remaining vegetables also placed lengthwise. Slice steak as thinly as possible across the grain. Lay beef strips across bed of greens. Add any accumulated beef drippings to the dressing and dribble over meat and greens. Garnish with lime wedges and sprigs of mint. Or for a crowd arrange on a long narrow platter as on the cover.

This Beef Salad is one of the most delicious Thai dishes I have ever tasted. It combines all the qualities I have loved about Thai food from the day I first tasted it: Beautiful appearance, a wonderfully interesting combination of flavors and textures, fresh ingredients, lots of vegetables but not too much meat. It is easy to prepare and can be done ahead of time. Thai salad dishes often are not served chilled but rather at room temperature making this one perfect for a buffet table.

thai hot bean salad

This gloriously colorful dish contains no meat, no onions and no garlic. Is it bland? No way! Dried hot pepper flakes that have been fried in oil until they darken take on a wonderfully toasty flavor. Don't overcook the beans — they should remain crunchy.

1/2	pound fresh whole string beans, stems trimmed
2	tablespoons peanut oil
2	teaspoons hot pepper flakes
1	tablespoon grated ginger
1	teaspoon grated lemon zest
1/3	cup coconut milk
1	tablespoon fish sauce (more or less to taste)
1	tablespoon oyster sauce
1	cup *each* finely shredded red cabbage and iceberg lettuce

Garnish: chopped peanuts, slices of orange or lime, radish "roses"

Fry pepper flakes in hot oil until they begin to darken (3 to 4 minutes.) Add ginger and lemon zest and cook 1 minute. Add beans and toss until they turn bright green. Add coconut milk, fish sauce and oyster sauce and heat thoroughly.

PRESENTATION Pour hot beans onto a bed of shredded lettuce and cabbage. Garnish as extravagantly as possible.

thai shrimp slaw

SERVES FOUR

Here are all the complex flavors and subtle surprises we associate with Thai food. Strict vegetarians can substitute cubed tofu for the shrimp. If you want more pungent flavor, use broccoli rabe (also called rapini) instead of bok choy, discarding the tough stems. The dressing contains no oil, making this an ideal dieters' dish. Of this, one could almost say the more you eat, the thinner you get!

1 1/4	pounds cooked medium shrimp
1	carrot, grated on diagonal into long threads
1	small red onion, thinly sliced vertically
1/2	head bok choy or broccoli rabe, finely sliced
1/2	head savoy cabbage, finely sliced

Garnish: 1/4 cup toasted sesame seeds, 1 small head of radicchio, finely sliced, slices of orange

---

wasabi dressing

Combine:

1/3	cup lime juice
2	tablespoons pickled red slivered ginger*
1	small hot chili pepper
2	teaspoons *each* dark sesame oil*, fish sauce* and sugar
1/2	teaspoon wasabi (green horseradish) powder*

PRESENTATION Prepare dressing and toss with remaining ingredients. Pile on platter and sprinkle with finely shredded radicchio and sesame seeds. Set orange slices around edge.

* These ingredients are easily found in any Asian market and many supermarkets.

gado gado

(front cover)

SERVES EIGHT

Here's a different way to use that trifle bowl that you only take out once a year — a layered salad.

Sometimes inspiration for meals comes from a beautiful or interesting serving piece. If you have a clear, straight-sided glass bowl, a salad bowl or even a clear soufflé dish, layered salads present an opportunity to create a beautiful mosaic, especially impressive for a party.

This delicious Malaysian vegetarian salad can be layered in a clear glass bowl or "composed" on a large, handsome platter. It is served with a hot peanut dressing — another interesting variation on the theme of cold salad/ hot dressing. Use the shredding and slicing blades of your food processor to prepare all the ingredients and prep time will be minimal. The egg pinwheels on top are a nice surprise. You can do everything ahead and reheat the dressing at serving time.

1	pound potatoes, cooked and cubed
1 1/2	cups red cabbage, diced in 1/3-inch cubes
1 1/2	cups baby carrots
1 1/2	cups bean sprouts (or alfalfa or radish sprouts)
1 1/2	cups shredded spinach, watercress or arugula
1 1/2	cups diced white radish (diakon) or red radishes
1 1/2	cups chopped green scallions
1 1/2	cups diced red peppers
4	eggs prepared as four thin omelette-crêpes, rolled up and sliced into 1/2 inch pinwheels
	diced fried tofu, if desired

chili-peanut dressing

2	tablespoons peanut oil
1	medium onion
2	cloves garlic
3	fresh green chili peppers, seeded and minced
1	teaspoon Chinese shrimp paste, Thai fish sauce or anchovy paste
1	tablespoon brown sugar
2	tablespoons lemon juice
2	cups coconut milk
3	tablespoons peanut butter
1	cup water
1	teaspoon salt

Sauté onion, garlic and chilies in oil until onion is wilted. Add remaining ingredients and simmer 3 to 4 minutes. Serve hot dressing over cold salad.

Garnish: 1 cup salted peanuts, coarsely chopped.

PRESENTATION Layer the ingredients in a handsome clear glass bowl, egg pinwheels on top, sprinkle with peanuts, cover with plastic wrap and chill well. Alternatively arrange the ingredients on a large platter. Serve hot dressing in a pitcher or gravy bowl with ladle.

chiffonade

Anything "chiffonade" means "finely shredded." A chiffonade of salad greens makes pretty layers that are easy to serve. For an "all-leaf" salad try a variety of different colored leafy layers in your clear glass bowl.

korean hot & cold roast pork

SERVES SIX

If you love pork but worry about calories and cholesterol, there's good news. Hog breeders have responded to public demand for less fatty meat by breeding skinnier pigs. Pork tenderloin is a tidy roast — often about the size and shape of your forearm — that comes trimmed to be 93 percent lean. It's small enough (about a pound and a half) to be easy to handle and quick to cook. This cut, like its beef counterpart, is wonderfully tender. Because overcooking makes pork dry and tough, use a meat thermometer. The roast will continue to cook a bit as it stands.

What makes this dish unusual is that the pan juices from the roast pork become the hot dressing that you dribble over the meat and salad greens.

sesame marinade

Combine:

1/2	cup soy sauce
3	tablespoons brown sugar
2	scallions, minced
2	cloves garlic, mashed
1	teaspoon grated ginger
1/2	teaspoon white pepper
2	tablespoons peanut oil
2/3	cup sesame seeds

1 1/2	pounds pork tenderloin, trimmed
1/4	cup vinegar
1/4	cup hot water

salad bed

Mixed shredded greens (any combination of lettuce, red cabbage, arugula, radicchio, Chinese cabbage, etc.) plus carrot, red cabbage and sprouts (alfalfa, soy, or radish.)

With a knife, slice lettuce into long shreds (what the French call "chiffonade.") Use a grater or processor to cut the cabbage and carrot into long shreds (place carrot lengthwise to blade.)

Marinate pork overnight. Remove meat from refrigerator 2 hours before meal time. Preheat oven to 350°. Place meat in small heavy pan and pour marinade over top. Roast for 45 minutes turning occasionally, or until internal temperature reaches 160°. Remove meat from pan, add vinegar and hot water to drippings and return pan to oven for 15 minutes.

PRESENTATION   Arrange a bed of greens and sprouts on plates. Place a line of shredded red cabbage down one side and shredded carrot down the other. Slice pork into 1/4 inch medallions. Arrange slices of meat overlapping down center and drizzle hot pan dressing over all.

pineapple rice salad

SERVES FOUR

This is a hot and cold salad: hot (temperature-wise) sausage, cool fruit. If you've never tasted Chinese sausage, you're in for a treat. If you happen to see them on the menu in a Chinese restaurant be sure to order that dish. You can often find them in the frozen food chest of Asian markets. They are dry, reddish, marbled, with a slightly sweet, mild flavor unlike any Western sausage. Believe me, I wouldn't suggest that you go to the trouble of finding them if it wasn't worth it. This dish can be made without Chinese sausage but don't substitute another kind. Choose a ripe, juicy pineapple. How to tell when a pineapple is ripe? Smell is a better indicator than firmness. If it has little or no pineapple smell, it won't taste good either.

3 to 4	Chinese sausages
1/2	pound cooked shrimp
1	tablespoon peanut oil
1/4	cup minced onion
1	clove garlic, mashed
1	egg
1	tablespoon soy sauce
1 1/2	cups cooked rice (Uncle Ben's preferred)
1/4	cup *each* golden raisins, flaked coconut, minced cilantro and minced scallion
1	small whole pineapple, cored, sliced in wedges and chilled

Garnish: lettuce and nasturtium leaves and flowers or rose petals

Simmer sausages in water to cover for 10 minutes. Slice thinly on diagonal and set aside. In non-stick pan, fry onion in oil until wilted, then add garlic and cook gently for a minute or two, stirring often. Add cooked rice and stir to mix. Place in a mixing bowl. Break an egg into same pan and scramble quickly just until set. Add to bowl. Add remaining ingredients except pineapple and sausage and toss to mix. Moisten with accumulated pineapple juice. Serve at room temperature.

PRESENTATION Arrange a few green leaves on plates. Pile rice on plates, surround with pineapple chunks and fresh flowers, if you have them. In microwave, re-heat sausage for 30 seconds or just until sizzling and arrange on top of rice. Top with sprigs of cilantro. Serve with Baby Blueberry Muffins (see Go-Withs.) Sorbet is a nice end to this meal.

spicy szechwan noodle salad

SERVES SIX

If you don't have Chinese chili paste on hand, it is easily obtained in any Asian market. This version is vegetarian, but if you wish you can top the noodles with shredded cooked chicken, diced ham, shrimp or crabmeat, moistened with a little dressing.

1	pound fresh Chinese wheat noodles or linguini, cooked *al dente* according to package directions

szechwan dressing

Combine:

1/4	cup *each* dark sesame oil, peanut oil, cold tea, soy sauce, vinegar, sherry
1	clove garlic, mashed
3	scallions, minced
2	teaspoons chili paste
1	tablespoon honey

Garnish: chopped cilantro, scallions, diced seeded cucumber, diced red pepper

Toss hot noodles in dressing, then refrigerate 1 hour or more to blend flavors.

PRESENTATION Arrange noodles on platter and sprinkle top with chopped cilantro, red pepper and cucumber. Lay several whole scallions and long sprigs of cilantro along one side of platter.

rumaki salad

bamboo skewers soaked in water for 1/2 hour

1   pound large scallops

1/2   pound smokey bacon

3   tablespoons soy sauce

1   package spinach, rinsed, drained and picked over or torn watercress, dandelion greens, arugula, endive, young red stem chard or other sturdy greens arranged on 4 plates.

Garnish: 4 small bunches of grapes or edible flowers

Preheat broiler. Marinate scallops in soy sauce while you partially cook bacon over very low heat until almost done. Remove bacon reserving fat and drain on paper towels. Discard scallop marinade and intertwine 2 scallops with bacon on each skewer. Cut skewers if too long. Broil close to heat source, turning once, for 10-12 minutes or just until scallops are opaque. Remove and tent with foil to keep warm.

lemon bacon dressing

Pour all but about 3 tablespoons bacon fat from pan and place pan over medium heat. Whisk together:

1   teaspoon corn starch

1/2   cup water

1/4   cup lemon juice

2   teaspoons sugar, or more to taste

1/2   teaspoon dry mustard

Add mixture to pan and cook stirring until thickened. Salt to taste.

PRESENTATION   Drizzle hot dressing over bed of greens on each plate and set 2 or 3 bacon/scallop skewers on top. Serve immediately.

Choose big, very fresh scallops for this dish. Smokey bacon, pre-cooked slowly over lowest heat, doesn't lose it's delicate flavor. A good hickory-smoked brand from the supermarket will do nicely but if you've never tried a real smoke house bacon you're missing a treat. Check the back of cooking magazines for mail order sources if you don't have a local smokehouse; or see page 8.

szechwan rainbow trout in aspic

SERVES FOUR

When dining in a Chinese restaurant, most people follow the Chinese custom of sharing dishes so that each diner samples a variety of entrées. Preparing a number of hot dishes at home may be more trouble than many cooks want to take on, however. Cold dishes make the job easy — they can be done ahead at your leisure. Although we don't usually associate cold foods with Chinese cooking, there are some wonderful examples. This one is a lovely dish that pairs well with cold noodle or rice salad. The poaching broth turns into a delicious aspic when chilled.

4	1/2-pound whole rainbow trout, cleaned, heads removed, tails on
1 1/4	cups water
1/3	cup light soy sauce
1	small onion, thinly sliced
2	teaspoons sesame oil
2	tablespoons vinegar
1	tablespoon sugar
1/2	teaspoon hot oil
1	tablespoon slivered ginger

Garnish: cilantro sprigs, scallion curls

Place all ingredients except trout in shallow pan. Bring to a boil, add trout and turn heat to lowest setting. Cover tightly and simmer gently for about 15 minutes, turning once. Do not overcook. Cool to room temperature. Remove skin from fish and trim any rough edges.

Lay fishes head to tail on oval platter with a raised lip. Strain broth over fish and set in refrigerator to chill several hours until broth is set or overnight.

PRESENTATION   Slice the green portion of one scallion into 2-inch lengths. Slice into slivers vertically. Drop into ice water for 15 minutes or until curled. Blot scallion curls and sprinkle over trout. Arrange cilantro sprigs around edge. Serve with Spicy Szechuan Noodle Salad (page 50.) Finish the meal with a bowl of fresh pineapple, chilled canned litchees (available in Asian markets,) sliced papaya and kiwi.

indonesian fruit & shrimp salad

SERVES FOUR

Papaya, cucumber, shrimp, orange, apple, hot peppers, cilantro, fish sauce, sesame oil and lime juice make a surprising combination for western palates. In Thailand, it's called yam chomphu. *In Java, this type of salad (called* rudjak*) is served on ritual occasions. Everything can be assembled ahead but add the cucumbers at the last minute because they tend to wilt in the dressing. Granny Smith apples stay crisp and don't discolor. The flavors of this dish are so stimulating and refreshing, I think it's the best light supper for a beastly hot day.*

2	**Granny Smith apples, in 1/2-inch cubes (do not peel)**
2	**oranges, sectioned**
1	**cup pineapple cubes**
1	**papaya, cubed (save some seeds)**
1	**pound cooked, peeled shrimp**

Serve this beautiful salad in a gorgeous leaf bowl that is surprisingly simple to create. Finely chiseled savoy cabbage is one of the most beautiful vegetables in the produce section. Just line a shallow bowl with four or five large outer leaves and reserve the rest of the cabbage for another use.

cilantro dressing

1/4	**cup minced cilantro**
2	**tablespoons fish sauce**
1	**tablespoon sesame oil**
1/4	**cup *each* sugar and lime juice**
	fresh minced jalapeño or red pepper flakes to taste

Pour dressing over fruit-shrimp mixture and refrigerate until well chilled.

At serving time add

1/2 **English cucumber, sliced (do not peel)**

Garnish: large outer leaves of savoy cabbage

TIP
To keep any fruit salad looking fresh longer, dissolve one vitamin C tablet in 1/4 cup water and toss with fruit. Ascorbic acid (vitamin C) keeps fruit from discoloring.

PRESENTATION Line a shallow bowl with several large outer leaves of savoy cabbage. Add sliced cucumber to fruit mixture, toss to coat and scoop mixture into the leaf-lined bowl. Garnish with threads of red cabbage or flowers, if you have them, and a sprinkling of papaya seeds. Serve with Honey Pecan Rolls (See Go-Withs.)

a *feast* in an ancient *p*ouch

PITA, THAT FLAT, round, chewy loaf now available all over the United States, was invented nine thousand years ago. Unleavened flat breads date back even earlier to the days of the cave man, but ancient Egyptians are credited with combining wheat flour and yeast to make the first raised flat breads. As it bakes, pita quickly develops a crust, trapping expanding air and gases from the yeast and forming the characteristic pocket. Dieters love pita bread because it is low in calories and so versatile. Pita pockets are an edible salad bowl – they can hold a humble tuna salad or the most creative combo you can dream up.

To my mind, however, the best pita fillings are based on the traditional Middle Eastern ones. High tech, hybrid American culture is half a world and eons away from Middle Eastern cultures which span thousands of years. Yet their ancient cuisines suit our health-conscious eating style and appease our longing for exotic, yet down-to-earth dishes.

The flavors of the Middle East are based on some of the most sophisticated yet simple combinations in the world. Lemon juice, fruity olive oil, garlic and onions are the pillars of an endless variety of superb cold salads.

One of my early "food epiphanies" occurred when I was a college student. A friend introduced me to a Middle Eastern restaurant, the Red Fez, which served the most delicious Greek-style salad I had ever tasted. My recipe (next page) is based on that superb creation, redolent with the flavors of olive, lemon, mint, oregano, and feta cheese. (Those plastic-boxed impostors in luncheonettes and take-out joints, with their tasteless canned olives, cider vinegar – never! – and flavorless oil, bear little resemblance to the real thing.)

We Americans have taken many other traditional Middle Eastern salads to our hearts. Included in this category are ground up "salads" like hummis (puréed chick peas) and baba ganoush (puréed eggplant.) To my mind most versions of these two miss the mark. Hummis should be distinctly lemony with a very faint perfume of cumin. Baba Ganoush should have a wisp of smoky taste, the result of broiling, or better yet grilling, the eggplant until the skin chars and blisters. I have purchased the latter in Armenian markets with a garnish of pomegranate seeds strewn on top. Very pretty. And we thought California cooks invented grilled vegetables!

In the last several years Tabooli, a wheat salad, has become commonplace in this country, available even in supermarket salad bars. My version is more complex than most but worth the trouble. And although I love tabooli, I pass along a favorite variation just for a change. It uses orzo, a rice shaped-pasta, instead of the usual cracked wheat and contains zucchini for crunch. Choose a fruity, extra virgin oil for all these dishes and use Mediterranean-style olives (i.e., Calamata, not California canned olives) and fresh mint if you have it. Taste frequently and feel free to alter proportions to suit yourself.

red fez salad

The secret for success of this salad depends on having all ingredients very crisp and icy cold. Serve in a chilled glass or ceramic—not wood—bowl. Wood does not chill well.

1	head *each* iceberg lettuce and red lettuce, rinsed, spun dry and torn into bite-size pieces. Chill in refrigerator until crisp
1	English cucumber, thinly sliced
1	bunch radishes, thinly sliced
2	ripe tomatoes, cut in 8ths
1/4	cup thinly sliced mild onion (such as Vidalia, Spanish, red or Texas 1015)
1/2	pound feta cheese, thinly sliced
1/2	pint black Mediterrean-style olives

lemon mint dressing

1/2	cup lemon juice
2/3	cup fruity olive oil
1	teaspoon dry oregano
1/4	cup minced fresh mint or 1 tablespoon dried
2	cloves garlic, mashed
1/2	teaspoon salt

Combine and chill for 1 hour. At meal time pour over salad, toss gently and serve.

pita fillings

orzo tabooli

Orzo is a rice-shaped pasta.

1	**cup orzo**
3	**small zucchini, sliced thin, then cut in half-moons**
1/4	**cup *each* olive oil and lemon juice**
1	**large ripe tomato, diced**
1/4	**cup *each* minced fresh mint, parsley, scallions and pitted olives**
1	**teaspoon dry oregano**
1/4	**cup toasted pignolis (pine nuts)**
1	**cup crumbled feta cheese**
	salt to taste

Cook orzo in a large pot of boiling water for about 8 minutes or until tender but still quite firm. Put cut zucchini in large bowl with strainer on top and pour orzo and cooking water into strainer. Lift off strainer with orzo and allow to drain. Let zucchini stand in hot water for 4 minutes then drain. Toast pignoli by stirring in a hot pan until lightly browned. In large bowl combine all ingredients reserving some tomato slices, cheese and olives for garnish. Chill well. Mound salad on lettuce leaves.

To serve Middle Eastern salads in pita breads, halve and open the loaves and spread the interior with plain yogurt (as you would spread mayonnaise.) Line with shredded lettuce, thinly sliced cucumber and tomato and fill with one or several salads. Or you can set out platters of fillings and bowls of dressings and a basket of warmed, split pita breads and invite diners to be creative. You won't miss the meat, but if you have die-hard carnivores in the crowd, grill chicken or lamb shish kebabs. Brush with olive oil and lemon juice while grilling.

baba ganoush
with yogurt

This dish is often called Poor Man's Caviar, but is beloved by poor and rich alike.

2	large eggplants
2	cloves garlic
1/4	cup tahini or olive oil
1/4	cup lemon juice
1/4	cup plain yogurt

Grill halved eggplants over coals or a gas grill or, cut side down, under the broiler until skin is charred and blistered and center is soft. Remove skin and squeeze as much juice as possible from pulp. Purée pulp in processor, adding remaining ingredients. Pour into a bowl and gently fold in yogurt. Sprinkle with minced parsley or pomegranate seeds.

---

lentil hummis

1 1/4	cups cooked, drained lentils
1/4	cup lemon juice
1	clove garlic
1/3	cup tahini or olive oil
	salt to taste
	small pinch of cumin or coriander

**Garnish: minced parsley and red oil made by mixing
1/2 teaspoon paprika with 1 tablespoon olive oil**

Purée all in a processor until very smooth, adding water as necessary to make a soft consistency.

Spoon into a pottery bowl, dribble a little red oil and sprinkle chopped parsley on top. Can be made with canned chick peas.

persian
poached
platter

Cold poached ingredients form the basis for this classic dish. The trick is to remove the vegetables from the poaching water while they are still crunchy, drain well and arrange them beautifully on a handsome dish. Use either dressing (right) or serve both in small pitchers or bowls at the table.

string beans	broccoli
cauliflower	zucchini
asparagus	yellow squash
baby turnips	carrots

Slice an assortment of vegetables into bite-sized pieces and poach in a large pot of boiling water to which you have added bouillon cubes or salt. Cook each kind individually and remove with a strainer when just *al dente*.

PRESENTATION Arrange cooled vegetables attractively on a platter. Add shredded lettuce, sliced tomatoes, thinly sliced mild onion and cold poached chicken breasts, shredded, if you want a little meat. Serve with Tarator or Tahini Dressing.

turkish tarator dressing

2	slices white bread, crust removed
1	cup walnuts, almonds *or* pine nuts (pignoli)
1/2	cup olive oil
1/4	cup wine vinegar *or* lemon juice *or* half and half of each
1 - 2	cloves garlic
	salt to taste

Moisten bread with a little water and squeeze dry. In processor, purée all ingredients until smooth and creamy.

tahini dressing

2	cloves garlic, mashed
1/2	cup *each* tahini and lemon juice pinch ground cumin
1/4	cup yogurt
1/4	cup parsley, chopped
	salt to taste

In processor, purée garlic, tahini, lemon juice and cumin until smooth. Add salt, yogurt and parsley and pulse once or twice.

★ *Tahini is a paste similar to peanut butter but made with sesame seeds. You can find it in Asian, Greek and Middle Eastern markets and many supermarkets.*

circassian chicken *with* white bean salad

SERVES FOUR

A favorite among Turks and Ukranians, this dish of cold chicken with walnut sauce is a classic. The delicate sauce is almost like a mayonnaise although it contains no oil. Poached chicken is the traditional benefactor of this velvety coating but you can use a rotisserie chicken from the deli or your own grilled chicken that has been basted with garlic and olive oil.

1	whole cooked chicken, boned and sliced
2	tablespoons *each* olive oil and lemon juice

white bean salad

Combine:

1	1-pound can white beans, rinsed and drained
1/4	cup *each* olive oil, lemon juice and finely minced scallion
1/2	cup finely minced parsley
	salt and pepper

Garnish: lettuce leaves, tomatoes and olives

walnut sauce

1 1/2	cups walnuts
1	tablespoon paprika
1/2	cup bread crumbs
1/2	onion powder
1 2/3 to 2	cups chicken bouillon
	salt to taste

Grind walnuts, paprika and bread crumbs in processor until very fine. Slowly add bouillon and continue processing until mixture is very smooth, adding more bouillon until consistency resembles soft whipped cream. Chill.

PRESENTATION   Line plates with lettuce. Moisten chicken slices with a bit of olive oil and lemon juice to make it glisten, arrange on lettuce and place a spoonful of bean salad, tomato slices and olives alongside. Spoon walnut sauce over chicken and sprinkle with paprika. An easy and surprisingly delicious dessert: Stew dried apricots in water to cover until soft, add a little kirsch or curaçao and chill well. Serve with a generous puff of whipped cream and strong coffee.

couscous salad

SERVES FOUR

Couscous is the most renowned dish of Morocco and with good reason. Here is a vegetarian salad version that's lighter but the flavors are just as exotic. Couscous, pronounced koosh-koosh by the natives, has a delicate taste and texture that is the perfect foil for the exciting textures, colors and flavors that make up this dish.

Combine:

8	ounces couscous, cooked according to package directions
1	cup canned garbanzos, rinsed
1	carrot cut in 1/4-inch dice
4	small redskin potatoes, cooked, cooled and cubed
1	medium zucchini, cut in 1/4-inch dice
6	radishes, thinly sliced
1	ripe tomato, diced
1/2	cup currants or raisins
1/2	cup Mediterranean-style olives
2	scallions, minced
1/2	cup minced cilantro or parsley

curry vinaigrette

Whisk together:

1/4	cup lemon juice
1/2	cup olive oil
1	clove garlic, mashed
1	teaspoon curry powder
1/2	teaspoon *each* white pepper and salt
1/4	teaspoon cinnamon

harissa

In processor, combine:

1	clove garlic
1/4	cup peanut butter
1/2	teaspoon *each* cumin and coriander
1	teaspoon paprika
1/4 to 1/2	teaspoon cayenne
	juice of l lemon
1/2	cup olive oil
	salt to taste
	water to make consistency of heavy cream

Garnish: curly greens, sweet potato chips, radish slices

PRESENTATION Pour dressing over couscous mixture and toss lightly. Chill 1 hour. Line plates with greens and pile couscous on top. Harissa is traditionally very hot. If you prefer something milder use less cayenne. Pass harissa in a small bowl for those who like some "bite" to their food. Slice 1 peeled sweet potato paper-thin on a mandoline. Soak in ice water 1 hour to make slices curl. Tuck around edge of dish. Stand thin slices of radish on end on top of couscous. Serve with warmed flour tortillas (these are very similar to the African breads that might accompany such a meal) and butter. Finish with sliced oranges flavored with curaçao.

taramasalata

Tarama is carp roe that is sold in small jars in Middle Eastern and Greek groceries. This traditional Greek fish roe salad is light and flavorful. Serve it with a hearty red wine. When I can get them I like to use big yellow tomatoes for their lovely color and sweet flavor. The greener and fruitier the olive oil the better.

2	cups coarse bread, crust removed, cut in small cubes
2	teaspoons water
6	ounces fish roe
1	scallion, white part only
1	clove garlic
1	cup extra virgin olive oil
	juice 1 lemon
	salt and white pepper to taste
1/4	cup finely minced flat-leaf parsley

Briefly whirl bread, water, roe, scallion, and garlic in processor until combined. With machine running, pour in olive oil in steady stream until mixture resembles mayonnaise. Add lemon juice and whirl until combined. Scoop into a handsome bowl, smooth top, sprinkle with parsley and chill 1 hour or overnight.

2	tomatoes, cut in wedges
2	hard-boiled eggs, cut in wedges
1	red onion, thinly sliced preferably on a mandoline
1	cup Calamata olives
1	lemon cut in wedges
3/4	pound cooked shrimp
1	large bunch watercress

a saucer of olive oil for dipping the bread

lemon vinaigrette

Combine:

1/4	cup lemon juice
1/2	cup olive oil
1	teaspoon oregano
1/2	teaspoon salt

PRESENTATION   Set bowl of taramasalata in center of a large platter and wreath with remaining ingredients. Drizzle "wreath" with lemon vinaigrette and serve with a basket of crusty peasant bread or very fresh pitas. Instead of butter with the bread serve fruity olive oil in shallow saucers for dipping. Finish with fresh figs and coffee granité (Freeze very strong, very sweet coffee and whirl in processor at serving time. Fill chilled demitasse cups and top with whipped cream and a dusting of unsweetened cocoa.)

lobster salad in the shell

This is the most festive salad I know, a perfect choice when you want to celebrate a special occasion or lift someone's spirits. I once made this for a friend in the hospital. She told me it was the best medicine she got. For every two people use three lobsters, so that each shell contains an abundant amount of meat. Adjust the proportions to fit the number of people you will be serving.

- 1 1/4 **pound lobsters, cooked and chilled**
- **Tender lettuce such as Boston or Bibb, or curly red or green lettuce**
- **Inner light-colored stalks of celery**
- **Tomatoes, standard size or cherry variety, whichever is riper and juicier**
- **Baby asparagus, of pencil thickness if available, cut to 6 inch length, steamed just until bright green and then quickly chilled**

If your fish market can steam the lobsters for you (many can, so ask,) by all means save yourself the trouble. Otherwise cook 1-1/4 pound lobsters in boiling water for about 12 minutes. Drain and cool. Pull off legs — these are yours to nibble on. With a sharp knife make a slit in belly. Remove meat and set aside. Using kitchen shears, cut away the belly shell leaving back intact. Cut into chest cavity and pull out contents. If there is coral inside, remove it and place it in a small bowl. (The coral will be bright red; it is the lobster's eggs so you will only find it in a female.) You may also reserve the greenish substance called tomalley. This is the liver. Some people consider this the very best part; others don't like it.

Remove claws, crack and pick out meat. Set whole claw meat aside for garnish. Dice tail meat. Using just the tender inner ribs, thinly slice celery on the diagonal, enough to make about 1/4 cup per lobster. Mash coral and mix with mayonnaise, about 1/4 cup per lobster. Add the tomalley too, if desired. Season with sour salt or lemon juice to taste. Add a dash of hot pepper sauce. Add diced lobster meat. Line lobster shell with a few shreds of lettuce to raise filling higher. Pile filling into shell. Chill for at least one hour.

PRESENTATION   For each portion, line a dinner plate with whole lettuce leaves, spoke fashion. Place whole lobster in center; sprinkle lightly with paprika and set claw meat on top. Arrange tomato slices on one side of plate. Lay asparagus along side of lobster. Just before serving, dribble greens and asparagus with lemon vinaigrette and sprinkle with sieved yolk.

Serve with corn on the cob and warmed yeast rolls. Champagne would be nice, too.

about
molded
salads

MOLDED GELATIN DISHES, also known as aspics, are less popular today than they were in our mothers' day. The quivering mounds of garishly colored and artificially flavored gelatin that were once so popular seem out of sync with today's tastes. It's too bad that enthusiasm for all molded dishes has declined, however. They are perfect for the way we eat today if we just omit the strident orange, lemon or cherry gelatin and substitute unflavored gelatin plus fruit or vegetable juices or bouillon. Molds have many virtues: They're fun to make, beautiful to look at, open to improvisation once you know the basics, festive, glamorous, easy, delicious and often low–cal. One more plus: They're a great way to use up leftovers.

Unflavored gelatin, a granular protein substance that comes in little packets, expands when it meets any liquid to become the architectural support for all manner of high-rise molded aspics. Before the turn of the century cooks laboriously made their own meat and fish jellies by boiling chicken feet, veal bones, hoofs and heads and fish skeletons. The process was tedious, not to mention unattractive, although the final results were often both beautiful and delicious.

Today we have but to tear open an inexpensive packet of innocuous unflavored gelatin to achieve in minutes the spectacular creations that formerly took days to prepare. Perhaps just because we take gelatin so much for granted, we have forgotten how really wonderful gelatin dishes can be. If lobster and caviar were cheap and commonplace, would they taste as good? Probably not.

I love the gleam of very clear aspic coating a layer of rosy salmon mousse or the brilliant garnet color of a cranberry ring holding creamy white turkey salad. A layer of decorated aspic glaze elevates potato salad from the commonplace to the sublime. Use your imagination to create your own variations. Contrary to popular belief, gelatin is not particularly tricky to work with. There are only a few principles you need to know to guarantee perfect results every time.

gelatin basics

■ One package of unflavored gelatin, about 1 tablespoon, will set 2 cups of liquid. The liquid can be just about anything — apple juice, tomato juice, chicken broth, bottled clam juice — or whatever combination you dream up. Chill the mixture until it becomes syrupy then fold in 2 to 3 cups of chopped ingredients — fruits, vegetables, cooked meat or fish. The only thing you can't use in an aspic is fresh pineapple which contains an enzyme that digests the gelatin.

■ To add gelatin, first soften it in about 1/4 cup of whatever liquid is called for in the recipe for about 5 minutes, then stir it over low heat until dissolved. Add remaining liquid to gelatin and stir to combine.

■ To ease removal of the aspic, rub the mold with a little vegetable oil. Because oil and water don't mix, the oil in the pan discourages the water-soaked gelatin particles from sticking. Don't use butter or spray vegetable coating which harden and hold the gelatin — just what you don't want. Alternatively you can rinse the mold with cold water which thins the gelatin at the point where it touches the mold and helps it to release.

■ To unmold, loosen edges with a thin knife. Rinse the serving plate with cold water. The moisture on the plate will help keep the aspic from sticking before you have a chance to center it. Dip the mold briefly into warm, NOT HOT, water. Place the moist plate upside down over the mold and flip both over. Shake gently, holding the mold firmly against the plate. Lift off mold. If the aspic does not release, dip again into warm water or wrap a towel dampened with hot water around mold.

potato salad in aspic glaze

SERVES SIX

Mix together:

2	cups diced hot cooked potatoes
1	tablespoon grated onion
2	tablespoons olive oil
3	tablespoons lemon juice
1 1/4	teaspoons salt

Combine:

1	package unflavored gelatin softened in 1/4 cup water
1	cup chicken bouillon, heated to boiling point
3	tablespoons white vinegar

Stir until gelatin is dissolved. Measure out 2/3 cup and add to it:

3	tablespoons water

Pour bouillon-water mixture into oiled 9"x 5"x 3" loaf pan and chill for a few minutes in freezer until almost set. Arrange in a decorative pattern over gelatin:

sliced olives	sliced hard-boiled egg
parsley sprigs	pimiento

Return loaf pan to refrigerator. Pour remaining bouillon mixture into a bowl and refrigerate until the consistency of unbeaten egg white. Whip with a whisk until frothy then fold in potato mixture and add

1/4	cup sliced radishes
1	cup minced celery
1/4	cup minced red pepper
1/3	cup mayonnaise
1/4	cup finely minced parsley

Spread over gelatin in loaf pan and chill until firm.

PRESENTATION Unmold on platter and surround with greens.

Never was potato salad so beautiful and elegant. Serve with a platter of cold cuts, assorted pickles and olives and good breads.

glazed salmon mousse

SERVES FOUR

A clear layer of aspic glazes the of pink salmon mousse underneath. Beautiful!
Serve with a bowl of dill-chive sauce.

clear aspic glaze

1	envelope unflavored gelatin
1/4	cup dry white wine
1 1/2	cups fish or chicken bouillon
1	teaspoon *each* sherry and lemon juice

Soften gelatin in wine then heat gently until dissolved. Add lemon juice and sherry and stir into bouillon.

2	cups fresh cooked or canned salmon, skinned and boned
1	envelope unflavored gelatin
1/2	cup cold water
1/2	cup heavy cream, whipped
1/4	cup mayonnaise
3	tablespoons lemon juice
1	teaspoon paprika
	salt, white pepper to taste

Mash salmon with a fork. Soften gelatin in water, then heat until dissolved. Whisk gelatin into mayonnaise, then add lemon juice and salmon. Fold in whipped cream.

Garnish: **paper thin slices of English cucumber, pimento strips, watercress or curly endive, lemon slices**

dill-chive sauce

1	cup sour cream
1/2	cup mayonnaise
1/8	cup *each* lemon juice, minced chives and minced dill
	salt and white pepper to taste

Wipe a thin coating of vegetable oil on inside of a 9-inch (about 1 quart) ring mold and chill mold. At the same time also chill clear aspic mixture in refrigerator until syrupy. Pour a thin coat of aspic into mold and swirl to coat all surfaces. Chill briefly (2 to 3 minutes) in freezer to set. Repeat process to build up two more layers. Dip pimento slices in aspic and arrange vertically around sides of mold. Chill briefly in freezer to set. Arrange overlapping slices of cucumber in a ring around base of mold. Pour a little more aspic over cucumber and briefly set in freezer to firm up. Spoon mousse into mold and return to refrigerator to chill.

PRESENTATION Unmold salmon ring on platter. Arrange greens and lemon slices around base. Set bowl of sauce in center of ring. Sprinkle sauce with a bit of chopped dill or chives.

molded clam gazpacho
with quick "grilled" chicken

SERVES FOUR

Hispanic cooking often combines poultry and shellfish (think of paella.) This dish combines the two in an unusual hot and cold salad. Prepare the molded gazpacho ahead and grill the chicken for 10 minutes at serving time.

1	envelope unflavored gelatin
1/2	cup cold water
1 1/4	cups clam-flavored tomato juice
1/4	teaspoon sour salt (or lemon juice to taste)
	hot sauce to taste
2	tablespoons vinegar
1	medium tomato, chopped
1/3	cup *each* chopped green pepper and peeled, seeded cucumber
1/4	cup finely minced mild onion
1	6-ounce can minced clams with juice

In small pan soften gelatin in cold water. Stir over medium heat until gelatin is completely dissolved. Add clam-tomato juice and juice drained from clams, sour salt and hot sauce. Chill stirring occasionally until mixture is the consistency of raw egg white. Fold in vegetables and clams. Fill four 6-ounce custard cups and chill.

quick "grilled" cumin chicken

1	whole cooked rotisserie chicken from deli

Combine:

1/4	cup *each* lime juice and olive oil
1	teaspoon *each* cumin and oregano
1/8	teaspoon cinnamon
	dash cayenne

Cut chicken into large slices and dip into lime juice mixture. Lay on a sheet of aluminum foil and broil or simply toast in toaster oven until piping hot (10 to 15 minutes.) Reserve extra marinade.

Garnish: finely shredded iceberg lettuce, cilantro

PRESENTATION Line plates with finely shredded lettuce. Unmold gazpacho on one side of plate and arrange warm chicken slices on other side. Combine any drippings from the chicken with reserved marinade and dribble over lettuce. Garnish with cilantro.

holiday cranberry mold *with* turkey salad

SERVES 8

A gorgeous, festive luncheon dish for the holidays (and a great way to use up leftover turkey.)

If you want the cranberry mold to be pink instead of red, use sour cream in place of the cold water. Wipe a thin coat of vegetable oil around the inside of the mold to prevent sticking or rinse it with cold water. The color of garnets, this old fashioned cranberry-laden gelatin mold celebrates the winter holidays beautifully. It's also a festive way to dress up leftover turkey. You'll need three or four oranges to use as ingredients and garnish.

cranberry mold

1	envelope unflavored gelatin
2	cups cranberry juice (1/4 cup cold, the rest heated to boiling)
2/3	cup sugar
1 1/2	cups ground fresh cranberries grated rind of one orange
1/8	teaspoon cloves
1/4	teaspoon cinnamon
1/2	cup chopped almonds
3	tablespoons sherry

Combine cranberries and sugar. Soften gelatin in 1/4 cup of cold cranberry juice. Heat 1 3/4 cup juice to boiling, add the softened gelatin and stir until dissolved. Add sherry, grated rind and spices. Refrigerate until partially set. Fold in cranberries and almonds, pour into an oiled 6-cup ring mold and chill until firm.

chunky turkey salad

This turkey salad is the best. The turkey is cut into big chunks, the celery is sliced very thin, and the mayonnaise dressing is made more luscious with the addition of sour cream.

6 to 8 cups cooked turkey, in 3/4- to 1-inch cubes

1 cup thinly sliced center stalks of celery

mayonnaise and sour cream in equal parts, to moisten

onion powder, salt and white pepper to taste

Garnish: orange zest, orange slices, ruffly lettuce

To unmold cranberry ring, loosen edges with paring knife, briefly dip mold into a pan of hot water, place a platter on top and, holding tight, quickly flip plate and mold together.

PRESENTATION Slice oranges into thick disks. With paring knife, cut evenly spaced notches into rind. Cut disks in half. Using a zester, peel long threads of rind from another orange. Arrange ruffled lettuce around mold and set "scallops" of orange slices around mold. Pile center high with turkey salad and sprinkle with orange zest.

lime shrimp cocktail *with* molded guacamole

Shrimp cocktail is good but not exciting. Guacamole, once considered exotic, has become commonplace all over the country. However this combination of the two is new, different, and "muy delicioso."

The whole thing can be made a day ahead and assembled at the last minute.

lime shrimp

Combine and chill for several hours.

1	pound cooked, shelled shrimp
1/4	cup lime juice
1/4	cup olive oil
1	teaspoon dried red pepper flakes
1/4	cup *each* finely minced red onion and cilantro
1/2	teaspoon salt

guacamole mold

2	envelopes unflavored gelatin
1	cup cold water
4	tablespoons lemon juice
3/4	teaspoon salt
1/2	teaspoon garlic powder
1/2	teaspoon hot sauce
4	medium avocados
1/4	cup finely chopped scallion or mild onion

In small pan, stir gelatin into cold water and let stand 1 minute to soften. Stir over medium heat until gelatin dissolves completely. Add salt, garlic powder, lemon juice and hot sauce. In processor, purée avocado with onion until smooth. Whisk avocado into gelatin mixture and pour into individual molds. Chill three hours or overnight.

Garnish: olives, finely shredded lettuce, thin slices of radish and cucumber, prepared salsa or homemade (see page 115 or Salsas.)

PRESENTATION Place a guacamole mold on each chilled plate and surround with shredded lettuce. Stand drained shrimp on end around molds and garnish with olives and vegetables. Dribble a bit of salsa over guacamole and some of the shrimp marinade over the lettuce. Serve with hot quesadillas (See Go-Withs.)

salmon salade niçoise

Invented in Nice, in the south of France, the classic Salade Niçoise uses canned tuna but I think cold poached salmon is so much more elegant. Good tomatoes are a necessity here. Use tomatoes from your garden or, if you must use purchased ones, choose fully ripe cherry tomatoes. Have all ingredients well-chilled.

4	hard-boiled eggs, quartered
1/2	pound whole green beans, stems only removed, blanched
8	small red potatoes, cooked and quartered
2	large ripe tomatoes, cut in eighths
1	pound cold poached salmon fillets, skinned and boned, broken into bite-size pieces
	red onion, sliced into paper-thin rings
	anchovy fillets
	capers
	oil-cured black olives

dijon vinaigrette

1	teaspoon Dijon mustard
1/4	cup wine vinegar
1/2	cup olive oil
	salt and freshly ground pepper to taste

Garnish: fresh herbs — rosemary, tarragon, basil or thyme

PRESENTATION   Some people toss this salad but I like it better "composed": On individual chilled plates, arrange each ingredient in neat piles. Drape one or two anchovies over the potatoes and sprinkle a few capers, onion rings and olives over all. Dribble with Dijon Vinaigrette, garnish with herbs and serve with good crusty bread, sweet butter and a bottle of red wine. Tastes even better outdoors.

spinach mushroom salad

SERVES FOUR

1	package fresh spinach, trimmed
1	package fresh mushrooms, washed and thickly sliced vertically
3	tablespoons butter
1/4	cup minced onion
1-2	cloves garlic, crushed
	home-made French bread croutons sautéed in olive oil

cottage cheese dressing

1/4	cup vinegar
1/2	cup olive oil
1/2	teaspoon salt
	freshly ground pepper
2/3	cup small curd cottage cheese

Whisk together oil and vinegar, stirring in seasonings and cottage cheese last.

Over high heat sauté mushrooms in butter until they just begin to "weep." Add the onion and continue cooking a minute more or until onion begins to wilt. Add garlic and immediately turn off heat. Set mixture aside to cool. Combine Cottage Cheese Dressing with cooled mushroom mixture.

PRESENTATION On large flat platter, arrange spinach leaves to cover. Spoon mushroom mixture on top. Top with croutons.

My mother served this on special occasions when I was a very small child. I remember I loved it then (odd, because spinach and mushrooms are not the sort of thing children tend to favor) and I love it now — as do guests whenever a special occasion arises. The nice thing about this dish is that it is hearty enough for a main dish when vegetarians and omnivores will be sharing the meal. On such occasions I also serve fried eggplant (see Go-Withs) layered with slices of fresh tomato and fresh mozzarella and topped with grated Asiago cheese. If you have confirmed meat-eaters at the table, you can slip in a few slices of prosciutto with the mozzarella, but generally nobody misses meat.

grilled portobellos in herb oil

SERVES FOUR

Portobello mushrooms are among the newer additions to our super-market produce departments. Earth brown, flat-topped and huge, these are the murky monsters of the mushroom family, growing as big as a small plate. They look impressive but that's nothing to how they taste. Until you taste this dish you will not know how good a mushroom can be.

Boston chef Michael Haggarty is the source of this fabulous recipe. He says that vegetarians (and even non-vegetarians) order these mush-rooms as a whole meal. It's easy to see why. They are meaty cutlets with a grilled flavor almost like steak. Allow one very large or two or more smaller mushrooms per person. The chef saves the stems for other uses but you can cut them into 3/4-inch sections and cook them along with the caps.

4	saucer-size portobello mushroom caps
1/2	cup herb oil (olive oil with chopped mixed herbs — rosemary, sage, thyme, parsley)

Brush mushroom caps liberally with herb oil and grill them over high heat for 3 to 4 minutes per side, or until they begin to char slightly, soften and release some of their juice. Remove to a platter and sprinkle with salt and lemon juice.

marinated olives

Rinse brine from Calamata olives and drain well. Coat with extra virgin olive oil and season with coarsely ground black pepper, crushed garlic, and threads of lemon and orange rind (use a zester to make these.)

PRESENTATION Line plates with frisée (finely curled endive) or mesclun (mixed tender greens.) Lay one or two grilled mushrooms on top and brush them with fruity olive oil to make surface glisten. Arrange several marinated olives alongside. Add a few roasted peppers for color, if desired. With a vegetable parer, shave flakes of Parmesan cheese over all. Add a homemade or purchased bread stick to complete the picture.

Button mushrooms taste best before their caps open up to reveal brown gills underneath. Portobellos, the big papas, however, are eaten when their gills are fully exposed. Because those gills act like sponges, they should never be washed in water. Just slice the cap from the stem, nip off the tip of the stem where it went into the ground, and brush away any debris with a damp towel.

scallop, salmon & baby pea terrines

SERVES TWO

3/4   pound scallops, rinsed, drained, patted dry

1   cup frozen petite peas, thawed

1   tablespoon egg white

2   tablespoons mayonnaise or heavy cream

1   teaspoon salt

1   pound skinless, boneless salmon fillet, cut in 1/2-inch cubes

Garnish: Boston lettuce and "tomato roses."

Purée all but the salmon in a processor until smooth. Turn into a bowl and fold in salmon cubes. Oil a muffin pan with 3-inch cups with spray coating. Fill cups with fish mixture almost to brim. Set muffin pan into larger pan and fill it with boiling water to a depth of about 1 inch. Bake at 375º for 25 to 30 minutes or until a knife inserted in the center of one cup comes out clean. Cool to room temperature. Place a jelly roll pan over the muffin pan and invert quickly. Discard excess liquid. Chill molds.

PRESENTATION Frost each mold with a mixture of half mayonnaise and half sour cream plus lemon juice to taste. Arrange a sprig of flat leaf parsley on top and place several capers beside it as "berries." Serve two apiece on a bed of tender lettuce leaves. Place a tomato "rose" on the side.

A lower calorie version of this: Substitute "lite" mayonnaise for regular and yogurt for sour cream or top with a salsa of finely minced cucumber, dill and chives in yogurt.

A lovely luncheon when served with Dutch Babies (see Go-Withs), purchased chocolate truffles and espresso.

When we think of molded salads we automatically think of gelatin. Not gelatin but the protein in the fish is what sets these lovely individual molds.

A light dish, pale green and pink and white, very pretty for a "ladies' luncheon." It tastes remarkably like lobster. Do ahead except for a quick garnish.

tomato roses

With a sharp paring knife, cut skin from tomato in one long spiral, ending at stem end. Curl up to form a rose. A great way to use those tough winter tomatoes. Save insides for soups or stews.

fresh tuna salad au poivre

Fresh tuna is a lot like swordfish but I like it even better. A deep red, meaty fish, tuna turns pale beige when cooked, making it easy to judge when it's done to your preference. Some people like it rare, like steak. However you prefer it, do not cook it past the point when it has changed color or it will be dry and taste like canned tuna. This recipe uses high heat and robust seasoning that would overwhelm a more delicate fish.

1	pound fresh tuna
2	tablespoons whole mustard seed
1	tablespoon whole peppercorns
1	teaspoon peanut oil
1	teaspoon coarse salt

Put mustard seed into a plastic sandwich bag and crush lightly with a rolling pin. Add peppercorns and do same. Rub mixture into tuna and set aside. Heat a heavy cast iron skillet very hot. Brush with oil. Sprinkle with salt and lay tuna steaks on salt. Cook on both sides just until the outside meat has lightened but there is a 1/4-inch band of darkness at the center. Remove from pan immediately. Cool completely then break into large chunks. Toss with

2 to 3	large ripe tomatoes, diced
2	teaspoons fresh rosemary or lemon thyme, minced
1/4	cup *each* lime juice and olive oil
1	teaspoon sugar

Chill 1 hour.

Garnish: mixed greens, nasturtiums, if you have them, long sprigs of herbs.

PRESENTATION Line platter with greens and mound tuna-tomato mixture on top. Arrange nasturtiums and sprigs of herbs around edge.

pink herring platter

SERVES TWO

*Not just slightly pink — HOT pink! A beautiful and unexpected color to find
on your dish.*

1	8-ounce jar herring in sour cream, coarsely chopped
2	red skin potatoes, cooked, peeled and diced
2	tablespoons vinegar
2	tablespoons minced red onion
1/4	cup "lite" sour cream
3/4	cup pickled beets, diced

Mix all together and chill for 1 hour.

Garnish: hard boiled eggs, quartered tomatoes, cucumber slices,
assorted pickles, carrot curls (lengthwise peelings immersed in
ice water)

PRESENTATION Cover each plate with curly endive or other
greens. Mound herring salad in center and surround with remaining
ingredients. Pass Creamy French Dressing (see Dressings), if desired.

Serve with the densest, darkest black bread you can find, warmed if
you please, or thin, crisp rye crackers, sweet butter and a good, frosty
beer. Warm apple crisp for dessert would be divine.

salmon fennel salad
with baked garlic aioli

SERVES FOUR

Aioli is traditionally made with raw garlic. While I love garlic, I don't like carrying it around with me for hours after the meal. Baking it as in this version gives it a mellower but still wonderful taste and it doesn't linger on your breath or in your taste buds.

1 1/2	pound salmon fillets, poached in broth of 1 cup bouillon and 1/2 cup dry white wine
2-3	heads radicchio, thinly sliced
1	bulb fresh fennel, thinly sliced vertically
1/3	cup capers

Garnish: fresh thyme or tarragon, lemon wedges, capers

baked garlic aioli

4	large cloves garlic
1	egg yolk
	juice of 1/2 lemon
	pinch of minced thyme
1/2 to 3/4	cup olive oil
	salt and white pepper

Dribble a tablespoon of oil over garlic and bake in a toaster-oven at 350° for about 25 minutes. Cool.

In processor whirl garlic, egg yolk and lemon juice until thick, about 10 seconds. With machine running, slowly dribble in oil in steady stream until mixture resembles mayonnaise. Season with salt and white pepper.

PRESENTATION Remove skin and bones from cooled salmon and break into chunks. Line plates with radicchio and fennel and top with salmon. Spoon aioli over top and sprinkle with capers. Garnish with long sprigs of fresh thyme (nice if it is in bloom) or parsley and lemon wedges.

pear, blue cheese & toasted nut salad

SERVES FOUR

The combination of cheese, fruit and nuts is a classic all over European and Mediterranean countries. The flavors are highly complementary and dishes containing them add up to far more than the sum of their parts. In my mother's Spanish family, a board with good cheeses, a bowl of beautiful fruit and a basket of nuts with a handsome nutcracker was set on the table as a final course to be lingered over, perhaps with a bit of madeira or sherry.

Here all are combined in a delicious salad. The sharp flavor of blue cheese combines especially well with the lusciousness of ripe pears. Choose any type of blue cheese. Each country has its own - English stilton, French roquefort, Italian gorgonzola. If you like a milder flavor, choose Danish Saga blue. Try apples and cheddar, another wonderful combo, for variety.

wine dressing

1/4	cup sherry, port or madeira wine
1/4	cup finely minced shallots
1	tablespoon vinegar
1/4	teaspoon salt
	dash white pepper
2	tablespoons walnut or peanut oil

Cook shallots in wine until reduced to a syrupy liquid. Whisk in remaining ingredients.

4	cups trimmed watercress
2	heads Belgian endive, sliced horizontally
2	pears thinly sliced
1/2	cup crumbled blue cheese
1/2	cup chopped, toasted walnuts, hazelnuts or pecans

PRESENTATION Toss greens with part of dressing and arrange on chilled plates. Toss pears in remaining dressing and arrange over greens. Sprinkle cheese and nuts over top. Serve with crusty peasant bread and a cup of hearty soup.

blushing passion chicken plate

(back cover)

This salad features lovely colors — golden slaw, pale green lettuce, sunny eggs — but it takes its name from the striking pink color of the dressing. Purchased rotisserie chickens cut down on preparation time. The ultra-creamy, golden slaw, by the way, contains neither onion nor mayonnaise. It's a variation on a James Beard recipe and is the best slaw I've ever tasted. Do the cranberry dressing and slaw the day before.

2	small cooked rotisserie chickens from the deli
2	heads of Boston lettuce
4	hard-boiled eggs

blushing passion dressing

2	cups cranberries
2	tablespoons horseradish
1/4	cup chopped red onion
1	teaspoon grated orange rind, optional
1	cup sour cream

In processor, grind onion and orange rind. Add cranberries and grind till finely chopped. Mix in sour cream and horseradish. Chill overnight. (Keeps indefinitely)

creamy gold coleslaw

1/2	cup salad oil or light olive oil
2	tablespoons flour
1/2	teaspoon salt
2	teaspoons dry mustard
	dash hot sauce
6	tablespoons sugar
1/2	wine vinegar
1	cup heavy cream mixed with 2 egg yolks
	grated cabbage, grated turnip and grated carrot, enough to make 8 to 9 cups

Heat together the oil, flour, salt, mustard, hot sauce, sugar and vinegar and stir until thickened. In small cup combine the yolks with the cream. Stir a bit of the oil mixture into the cream mixture, then add back to the oil mixture. Continue cooking and stirring until thick. Pour hot dressing over vegetables and allow to cool, then chill.

This can be made with all cabbage and enough carrot to color but the yellow turnip provides a pleasantly different taste and a beautiful color.

PRESENTATION Arrange lettuce leaves on 4 plates. Slice chicken, arrange on lettuce and spoon a line of dressing over slices. Spoon slaw into a lettuce cup. Garnish with slices of hard-boiled egg. Serve with warmed French bread or Quick Yeast Rolls (see Go-Withs)

THE LOWLY SHALL BE EXALTED

It's interesting to see how our tastes have changed in the past few years as we've become more aware of the effect of diet on illnesses like heart disease and cancer. Our affluence allows us to gorge ourselves on an unlimited supply of foods loaded with complete proteins — meat, poultry, fish and dairy products. A diet rich in buttery cheeses, gravy-laden chicken and fat-marbled steak, however, is no longer a sign of affluence and privilege but of foolhardiness.

Ironically, many of today's fashionably healthy dishes were once peasant foods. "Poor peoples'" dishes based on combinations of grains (such as wheat, corn, and rice) and legumes (beans) compensated for a scarcity of meats, poultry, fish and dairy products which contain high-quality protein. Combining grains and legumes creates a vegetable protein as complete as animal protein but without the drawbacks. Today we know that peasant fare is good for us because it is high in complex carbohydrates and low in fat and cholesterol. (Vegetables *never* contain cholesterol because cholesterol is an animal product although some do contain saturated fats.) So now we have reversed the proportions of the foods we serve: little meat, lots of "carbs."

The Chinese have eaten this way for centuries. Even Chinese-Americans often eat what to us would seem like huge amounts of rice every day (as much as two cups each meal.) Meat, fish and poultry are added as flavorings rather than as the main feature. Rice alone is an incomplete protein, but the addition of small amounts of foods containing complete protein supplies what's missing. Tofu, made from soy beans, while adding nothing in the flavor department, does the same because soy beans are one of the relatively few complete protein foods found in the plant kingdom.

Grains and beans, in fact, are the basis of many diverse culinary traditions. Creole cooks in Louisiana proudly serve red beans on rice, Brazilians eat black beans with theirs and all over the South, everybody eats Hoppin' John (black-eyed peas and rice) with corn bread. Hoppin' John, in fact, is traditionally eaten on New Years' Day to bring good fortune in the coming year. For each of these dishes there are as many recipes as there are cooks, and each cook takes pride in having the best and most authentic recipe.

pasta fazool salad

SERVES FOUR

Pasta and beans, in Italian "Pasta e Fagiole," sometimes pronounced "pasta fazool," is a peasant dish as common in Italy as macaroni and cheese in this country. The combination of grain (the wheat in the pasta) and legume (the beans) makes a flavorful, satisfying, nourishing meal.

8	ounces ditalini (also called chili mac pasta,) cooked and drained
1	15-ounce can canellini beans, drained and rinsed
1/2	cup fruity olive oil
2	cloves garlic, mashed
1/4	cup wine vinegar
1/3	cup minced flat leaf parsley
3	anchovy fillets, mashed

Garnish: tomatoes, lettuce, olives and pepperoncini

Heat together olive oil and garlic, stirring constantly until garlic turns pale gold. Add vinegar, anchovies, parsley, salt and pepper to taste. Pour mixture over pasta. Toss, add canellini beans and toss gently. Chill well to meld flavors.

PRESENTATION Line chilled plates with lettuce, slice tomatoes thinly and arrange across one side. Pile salad mixture in center and garnish with pepperoncini, additional anchovies, if desired, and olives.

using your noodle:
PASTA SALADS

Pasta salads were the height of fashion about a decade ago. Before that, to most Americans the word pasta brought to mind spaghetti or macaroni steaming under a tomato or cheese sauce. Unfortunately, today the words pasta salad often bring to mind the salad bar's soggy rotini awash in oily garlic dressing. Once combined on a recipe, pasta continues to absorb dressing and juices given off by whatever vegetables it is paired with. Within a few hours it is no longer al dente; it is soggy. For best taste and texture, serve pasta salad about an hour after preparation.

creamy macaroni salad
with olives

SERVES FOUR

Some things are so basic that a recipe seems superfluous. The eternally popular Macaroni Salad is about as down-to-earth as you can get. However, from sampling this offering at innumerable salad bars, I've learned that not all macaroni salad is the same and not all is good. This version has been a summer staple in my family and my catering business for more years than I can count. It's very creamy thanks to the finely chopped hard boiled eggs which hold the mayonnaise and yogurt dressing (less caloric than all mayonnaise.) The use of olives and the brine in which the olives are packed add an essential sharpness. This humble salad is a summer essential for me.

1/2	pound elbow macaroni, cooked and drained
1/2	cup mayonnaise
1/3	cup yogurt
1/2	cup pimento-stuffed green olives, halved
1/4	cup olive brine
1/3	cup finely minced mild onion
6	hard-boiled eggs
2 to 3	ribs celery, diced
2	tablespoons vinegar
1/4	cup minced parsley
	salt and fresh black pepper

Garnish: quartered eggs, sliced tomatoes, whole olives, parsley or celery leaves

Whirl 4 of the hard boiled eggs in a processor until minced. Quarter the other two and set aside. Combine all other ingredients.

PRESENTATION Pile macaroni into a lettuce-lined bowl. Garnish with quartered eggs, tomatoes, parsley and olives, cover with plastic wrap and chill one hour. Serve with a platter of cold sliced ham and chicken (from the deli) and hot cornbread.

grilled orange-mint chicken on fine noodles

SERVES FOUR

This the most delicate pasta salad I know. It combines grilled chicken (kept moist and succulent by overnight marinating) with tender fine egg noodles in a lovely orange-mint cream dressing. Very unusual, very beautiful, very easy.

1 1/2	pounds skinless, boneless chicken breasts
1/2	cup orange juice
1/2	cup oil
1	teaspoon salt
2	scallions, minced

Marinate chicken overnight. Grill over coals or broil 3 to 4 minutes per side or just until done. Do not overcook or meat will be dry. Set aside.

pasta

8	ounces fine egg noodles, cooked according to package directions
1	teaspoon each butter and salad oil
1	tablespoon finely chopped mint

Toss hot cooked noodles with butter, oil and mint. Set aside.

Garnish: orange zest, mint, salted almonds, 2 oranges, sliced

PRESENTATION Arrange soft (Boston or Bibb) lettuce on plates. Pour half of dressing over pasta and toss to coat. Arrange a nest of pasta in center. Peel 2 oranges and slice horizontally, then in half. Slice grilled chicken breasts on diagonal and alternate with orange slices on nests. Add any accumulated orange juice to dressing and dribble remaining dressing over chicken. Sprinkle reserved orange zest and chopped almonds over all. Garnish with sprigs of mint.

orange cream dressing

1/4	cup minced shallot or mild onion
3/4	cup dry white wine
1	orange, rind and pulp
1	cup heavy cream
1/2	teaspoon salt

Using a zester, pull long threads of peel from orange (or grate coarsely.) With paring knife, peel white pith from orange and slice into half moons. Set aside.

Combine wine, shallots and one-half the orange rind in small heavy pan. Boil until reduced to about 1/4 cup. Purée in food processor and return to pan with heavy cream and salt. Simmer 5 minutes. Cool.

riotous bean salad

SERVES FOUR TO SIX

This salad is a riot of colors and textures. It is the classiest version of three bean salad you will ever see and a complete meal in itself. To keep the canned beans from breaking apart, add them last and fold in gently.

1	package frozen baby peas, thawed
1	package frozen corn, thawed
1	red pepper, diced
2	ribs celery, diced
3	scallions, minced
1	carrot, diced
1/2	cup minced cilantro
1	1-pound can black beans, rinsed and drained
1	1-pound can cannelloni beans, rinsed and drained
1	1-pound can dark red kidney beans, rinsed and drained

Garnish: lettuce leaves or shredded purple cabbage

Combine the fresh and frozen vegetables and toss with the dressing. When well mixed, gently fold in the beans. Chill several hours to blend flavors.

spicy cumin vinaigrette

1/4	cup vinegar
1/2	cup olive oil
1/2	teaspoon salt
1	clove garlic, mashed
1/2	teaspoon cumin
1/2	teaspoon oregano
1/2	teaspoon hot sauce

PRESENTATION Line a platter with lettuce leaves or shredded purple cabbage (or both) and top with bean salad. Serve with hot biscuits or cornbread.

crab tutti frutti

SERVES FOUR

*Crab and fruit combine beautifully in this pretty salad. Fold the crabmeat
into the fruit with a light hand to keep the lumps from breaking apart.*

1   cantaloupe, sliced into 1/2-inch wedges

Combine:

1   cup orange sections
1   cup crushed pineapple
2   cups finely shredded cabbage
1   teaspoon grated orange peel
2   tablespoons lemon juice
1/4   cup salad oil
         pinch salt
3/4   pound lump crabmeat

Garnish: small lettuce leaves, mayonnaise,
2 hard-boiled eggs, sieved

PRESENTATION   Fan several melon sections on one side of
each of 4 plates. Fan small lettuce leaves on other side of plates. Pile
crab mixture in center. Place a dab of mayonnaise on top and sprinkle
with sieved egg.

grilled asparagus *with* smoked salmon

A beautiful composed salad that requires minimum cooking — just the asparagus and scallions. Ready-to-serve salmon slices and cheese complete the plate. You can use smoked salmon or Nova lox. Although both are expensive, you need less than a half pound to generously feed 4 people.

1/2	pound (about) smoked salmon or Nova lox
1/4	pound mild white cheese such as goat cheese, explorateur or brie
1	bunch of asparagus, trimmed
4	scallions trimmed to length of asparagus
3	tablespoons *each* olive oil and balsamic vinegar
1	whole clove garlic, skin on, mashed with flat side of knife
	salt to taste

Garnish: A few leaves of greens such as red stem chard or arugula

Heat oil with garlic in large, non-corrosive skillet about 4 minutes. Remove garlic. Add asparagus and scallions, salt to taste and gently toss vegetables in oil over high heat until lightly browned and just tender. Remove from pan and set aside to cool. Add vinegar to pan juices and swirl to loosen any clinging bits. Make bundles of asparagus and scallion and wrap in slices of salmon.

PRESENTATION Arrange asparagus bundles over greens on individual plates. Drizzle with oil and vinegar pan mixture. Set a cube of cheese alongside. Serve with piping hot Potatoes Caroline (see Go-Withs) and crusty whole grain bread for spreading with cheese.

brandade de morue

SERVES FOUR

1	pound fresh cod, skinned and boned, cut in chunks
2	cloves garlic
1/2	cup light cream
1/3	cup olive oil
1/4	cup lemon juice
	nutmeg, salt and white pepper to taste

Simmer cod in water to cover just until cooked through. In processor purée cod with garlic until smooth, adding cream and oil a dribble at time. Add lemon juice to taste and season with salt and pepper and a tiny bit of nutmeg. Chill.

1	large bunch watercress
1	box yellow pear tomatoes or cherry tomatoes
	oil-cured or Niçoise olives
	pimiento

Garnish: rosemary croutons – To make, slice French bread, brush with olive oil and sprinkle with rosemary. Toast in toaster oven until lightly browned.

lemon garlic vinaigrette

1/4 cup lemon juice	1/2 clove garlic
1/2 cup olive oil	1/2 teaspoon thyme
1/2 teaspoon salt	1 teaspoon hot water

Whirl in processor until combined.

This wonderful French dish should be more familiar than it is. In the days before refrigeration, it was made with dried salt cod. Today, fresh cod is readily available at a lesser price than its salty cousin. This version is almost mousse-like in texture, with a lovely garlicky, lemony flavor. When I served this to a friend who has travelled extensively in France, she closed her eyes and groaned with pleasure.

PRESENTATION Arrange watercress, tomatoes and olives on one side of plate. Dribble with dressing. Place a scoop of brandade de morue on other side and criss-cross pimiento on top. Set crouton along side. Diners spread the cod mixture on the crouton or eat with a fork.

meat and potato salad

SERVES FOUR OR MORE

This is a substantial dish, a good choice for a weekend supper watching football in front of the TV. Serve raw vegetable chips with Alsatian Cottage Cheese Spread (see Go-withs) for dieters; potato chips and corn chips for the reckless.

1 1/4 pounds thickly sliced roast beef from deli counter

Combine:

2	pounds about cooked small red-skinned potatoes, cubed
4	ounces crumbled blue cheese
1/4	cup each chopped red pepper and minced scallion
1	cup diced celery
1/2	cup pitted California black olives
1/3	cup olive oil
1/3	cup red wine vinegar
	salt and pepper to taste

Garnish: pickles, potato and tortilla chips, vegetable chips, lettuce leaves

Huge raw vegetable "chips" are deliciously crisp. Big root vegetables such as turnip, rutabaga, beet, sweet potato, jícama, daikon and black radish lend themselves to this treatment. Use a mandoline to make paper thin slices of vegetables. Immerse them in ice water for several hours to curl them into fanciful shapes. Use a few as garnish or do a variety to serve with dips.

PRESENTATION Spoon potato salad onto beef slices and roll up. Place one or two leaves of lettuce on each plate and top with beef rolls. Garnish with pickles, chips and serve with hot garlic bread and cold beer.

ham divan

(front cover)

SERVES FOUR

1   bunch broccoli

3/4   pound sliced deli ham, preferably a round ham
for easy folding

your favorite spread — honey mustard, chutney or hot
pepper jelly

Garnish: minced red bell pepper

Bring a large pot of water to a full boil. Add about 1 tablespoon salt.
Cut stalks from broccoli leaving about 2 inches. Peel the thick outer
skin from larger sections. Slice the heads into "trees." Drop broccoli
into rapidly boiling water. Keep heat on high. As soon as broccoli turns
bright green, drain it in a colander. Refill the pot with cold tap water and
immediately immerse the broccoli to stop the cooking process. Drain
and spin in salad spinner. Chill.

snow cap dressing

1/2   cup sour cream

1/2   cup mayonnaise

1/2   teaspoon onion powder

1/2   teaspoon garlic powder

2-3   tablespoons lemon juice

Combine sour cream or yogurt with mayonnaise.
Add seasonings and chill.

PRESENTATION   On an oval platter, arrange broccoli spears
around edge. To make ham "ruffles," place a dab of your choice of spread
in center of slice and fold in half, then in quarters.

Tuck "ruffles" in center. Dribble a line of dressing over broccoli.
Sprinkle with minced red pepper or paprika.

Serve with buttered hot popovers or biscuits. If you wish, add a little
Parmesan cheese to the batter for either one.

*I love meals that combine
prepared ingredients with those
you cook yourself. Ham Divan
(shown on the cover) is one of my
favorites also because the colors
are gorgeous: pink ham, dark
green broccoli, minced red pepper
and a snow white dressing. The
trick is to choose top quality ham
from your favorite deli counter
(economical because a little goes
a long way) and have it sliced
thinly. Ask for a taste if you're
not sure which ham is best.
This dressing is smooth and
creamy with a delicate, lemony
flavor. Use "lite" sour cream
or substitute yogurt (or use a
combination) if you want
to trim calories.*

99

green goddess prawn salad

This quintessential California salad was popular about 25 years ago but has been neglected of late. It's well worth reviving.

1	head romaine, torn into bite-size pieces
1 1/2	pounds cooked large shrimp, shells off, tails on
1	cup small homemade croutons (sourdough bread diced, browned in olive oil and tossed with a little Parmesan cheese)

green goddess dressing

8	anchovy fillets
1	scallion
1	small clove garlic
1/4	cup minced parsley
1	teaspoon dry tarragon
2	tablespoons lemon juice
3/4	cup sour cream
1 1/2	cups mayonnaise
1/4	cup tarragon vinegar

Purée all in processor. Chill to blend flavors.

Garnish: halved cherry tomatoes, California ripe black olives

PRESENTATION Line chilled plates with torn romaine. Arrange shrimp on top and spoon dressing over greens and shrimp. Toss a few croutons on top and garnish with tomatoes and black olives.
Serve with warmed sourdough bread and sweet butter.

beef & asparagus salad *with* hot dressing

SERVES FOUR

Serve this unusual salad at room temperature except for the dressing which is poured on piping hot.

1 1/4	pounds roast or corned beef (from deli or leftovers), sliced
1	bunch asparagus, cooked
10	small red-skinned potatoes, cooked and sliced
1	small head of escarole, torn into bite-size pieces

hot french dressing

Heat together just before serving (do not cook):

1/4	cup wine vinegar
1/2	cup olive oil
1/2	teaspoon salt
1	teaspoon Dijon mustard
2	hard-boiled eggs chopped
1	tablespoon *each* minced celery leaves, parsley and chives
2	teaspoons Worcestershire sauce

PRESENTATION   Line plates with torn escarole. Arrange meat, potatoes and asparagus on plates. Dribble hot dressing over all. Serve with rye bread and sweet butter.

the fickle puff

Several years ago, a certain biscuit mix company published a recipe for a puff pastry "bowl" which was filled with salad. The egg/butter/biscuit-mix batter was spread on the bottom, but not the sides, of a pie pan. When baked it formed a handsome golden brown bowl — sometimes. My problem was that I could never count on the puff to come out in a bowl shape, not a good feature because catering customers expect consistency. Sometimes the rim rose more on one side than the other, sometimes the bottom pulled away from the pie pan and formed an unsightly mountain right where I wanted a valley. I tried spreading the batter up the sides of various pans but reliable results still eluded me.

The biscuit mix company's recipe was nothing more than the standard cream puff (pâte à chou) but with mix in place of plain flour, a variation that produces no discernable improvement. I tried both the mix version and the traditional one, but the irregular shape problem persisted in both. Finally, I found the solution: Flat Is Reliable. I spread a circle of batter on a cookie sheet then split the baked disk into two layers and served it with the filling peeking out enticingly in between. You can use almost any salad filling imaginable, but I include a couple of delicious ones to get you started. For individual servings, make the traditional cream puff size and shape.

puff layers

1	cup water
5	tablespoons butter or margarine
1/4	teaspoon salt
1	cup flour
4	eggs

Bring water and butter to a boil. Add salt then add flour all at once, stirring vigorously until mixture forms a smooth ball. Remove from heat and let stand 1 minute. Add eggs one at a time, beating hard until each is mixed in. Grease a cookie sheet and dust lightly with flour. Lay a 9-inch plate upside down in center and draw its outline with a toothpick. Spread puff mixture in outline and bake 40 minutes at 400°. Turn off oven, split layers, pull out soft dough and return layers to oven, cut side up, to dry for 10 minutes.

new orleans seafood remoulade in a puff

SERVES SIX

Buy the crab and shrimp already cooked.

1	baked puff (preceding page)
8	ounces fresh crabmeat
1	pound cooked, peeled medium shrimp
1	head ruffled lettuce

remoulade

1/2	cup mayonnaise
1/2	cup sour cream
2	tablespoons *each* ketchup, lemon juice, minced scallions and capers
1	teaspoon *each* dry mustard, Worcestershire, and prepared horseradish
1/2	teaspoon tarragon
	dash hot sauce

Mix all together and chill for at least 1 hour to blend flavors.

Garnish: hard boiled eggs, cherry tomatoes, cucumber slices, radish roses and small sweet gherkin pickles.

PRESENTATION: Line the bottom layer of baked puff with ruffled lettuce leaves, letting ruffles extend 1 inch beyond edge. Pile on crab mixture. Add another layer of lettuce ruffles. Set puff layer on top. Place 8 bamboo skewers evenly around top to hold layers together. Cut skewers leaving 1/4 inch protruding. Press a bit of watercress and an olive or tiny tomato on each skewer tip. Around edge of platter arrange a wreath of watercress and lettuce dotted with quartered hard boiled eggs cucumber, tomatoes, radishes and pickles. Serve with iced tea and hot Cinnamon Pecan Muffins. (see Go-Withs)

basteela salad in puff layers

SERVES SIX

Basteela , a spicy chicken and egg filling baked in layers of thin pastry and glazed with sugar, is the Moroccan national dish. This cold filling draws on the flavors of that classic.

1	baked puff (page 102)
4	cups cooked diced chicken breast
4	hard boiled eggs, chopped
2	tablespoon lemon juice
1/2	cup *each* sour cream and mayonnaise
1/2	cup *each* minced parsley and chopped scallions
1/4	teaspoon cinnamon
1/2	teaspoon *each* white pepper, salt and dry ginger
1/2	cup *each* dried currants and chopped salted cocktail-type almonds

Reserve chopped almonds. Mix all ingredients together and chill for at least 1 hour to blend flavors.

In small heavy skillet heat 1/3 cup sugar until melted and rich golden brown. Add 1 tablespoon of the chopped almonds and dribble over top layer of puff, spreading quickly with knife.

Garnish: fresh mint, seedless grapes, apricots or figs (fresh or canned.)

PRESENTATION   Line the bottom layer of puff with ruffled lettuce leaves, letting ruffles extend beyond edge. Fold remaining almonds into salad at last minute (so they don't soften) then spread mixture on lettuce. Set glazed layer on top. Around edge arrange mint and fruit.

wilted spinach salad *with* chicken livers

SERVES FOUR

If you like chicken livers, you will love this salad. It has a Pennsylvania Dutch flavor because of the sweet and sour bacon dressing. It always brings raves. Tip: don't overcook the livers or they will become grainy. Use your largest skillet so that livers will brown quickly rather than boil in the copious juices they give off.

6	slices bacon, cut crosswise into 1-inch pieces
1	pound chicken livers
1/2	cup wine vinegar
3	tablespoons sugar
2	tablespoons ketchup
1/4	cup minced onion
1	10-ounce bag spinach, washed and trimmed

In large skillet, fry bacon until crisp and remove. Turn heat to high. Add livers to drippings in pan and sauté until livers are cooked but still pink inside. Remove livers and set aside. Add vinegar, sugar, ketchup and onion to pan drippings and bring to a boil, scraping up crusty bits as you stir. Return livers to pan to briefly reheat.

PRESENTATION Line a large bowl with spinach. Pour hot livers and sauce over spinach. Toss lightly to mix and sprinkle with bacon. Serve immediately.

cajun beef & shrimp salad

A hearty, flavorful salad that is perfect when you want to cook ahead.
Grill on an iron skillet as below, or over coals.

3/4	**pound shelled raw shrimp, tails on**
4	**4-ounce steaks, trimmed**
1/3	**cup Cajun blackening seasoning** **mixed with 1/4 cup peanut or vegetable oil**

Coat shrimp and steaks heavily with seasoning mixture. Heat an iron skillet piping hot. Grease skillet by rubbing with a piece of fat trimmed from the steaks, lower heat and sear shrimp on both sides until pink. Remove shrimp, rub pan with fat again and sear steaks on both sides. Turn heat down and continue cooking steaks to desired degree of doneness. Set shrimp and steaks aside to cool or refrigerate until serving time.

Prepare a chiffonade (thin strips) of mixed greens including a mild lettuce and flavorful greens such as

	arugula, radicchio or young mustard greens.
1	**small sweet onion, sliced thin**
1	**large tomato, sliced in thin wedges**

roquefort-mustard dressing

4	ounces Roquefort cheese
1/3	cup oil
1/4	cup wine vinegar
1	clove garlic, crushed
1	tablespoon Creole (coarse grained) mustard
1	teaspoon tarragon or thyme

Shake together in jar with a tight fitting lid (a canning jar works well.)

PRESENTATION Pile chiffonade of greens on plates. Slice meat into 3/4 inch cubes and arrange with shrimp over greens. Arrange tomato wedges and onion slices along side. Dribble with dressing and serve immediately with warmed crusty French rolls. Crème brûlée or New Orleans bread pudding with bourbon sauce for dessert, anyone?

24-hour crunch salad

A real beauty when layered in a deep clear glass bowl. This salad has made the rounds for many years so that now I think it qualifies as a classic. As the name implies, it is made a day ahead. Earlier versions called for iceberg lettuce which has an appealing crunchiness. However, iceberg lettuce also has a nasty habit of getting "rusty"; the cut edges take on an unattractive brownish-red discoloration after a day or so. I prefer to use romaine which, treated as below, duplicates iceberg's crunch but with more flavor and color — and it doesn't rust.

2	small heads romaine lettuce, sliced across the head into 1/2 inch strips, soaked in ice water and spun dry.

confetti mixture

1	diced red pepper
2	thinly sliced small carrots
5	chopped scallions
1	can diced water chestnuts
1	cup sliced black olives
1	cup sliced celery
1/2	cup sliced radishes
1	pound cooked shrimp

1	box cherry tomatoes, sliced horizontally in half
2	10-ounce packages frozen tiny peas, thawed and rinsed
2	cups grated cheese: cheddar, Swiss or blue
1/2	pound bacon cooked, drained and crumbled

sour cream chive dressing

1	cup mayonnaise
1	8-ounce carton sour cream
1/4	cup finely minced chives or scallions
1/2	teaspoon sour salt or lemon juice to taste

You can use "lite" mayonnaise and "lite" sour cream or use part yogurt, if you're concerned about calories.

PRESENTATION Make a ring of tomatoes around base of bowl, cut side toward glass. Layer one half of the shredded lettuce in bottom of bowl. Stand shrimp around sides of bowl. Chop remaining tomatoes and add to confetti mixture. Layer confetti mixture over lettuce. Add another layer of lettuce and the peas. The bowl should be full to within 1 inch of the top. Spread dressing over peas, sealing the edges and sprinkle with cheese and then bacon. Do not mix. Cover with plastic wrap and refrigerate overnight.

vegetarian 24-hour crunch salad (on back cover) Omit shrimp and bacon and proceed as above. Chop tomatoes and add as a layer. Cut a thin slice across the middle of a head of purple cabbage and place on top of sour cream dressing. The cabbage resembles a huge purple flower.

ensalada de seviche

(front cover)

SERVES FOUR

1 1/4	pounds large scallops, very fresh, sliced thin, horizontally
3/4	cup lime juice
1/4	cup thinly sliced mild onion, such as Vidalia or Spanish
1/2	teaspoon dried hot pepper flakes
1/2	teaspoon salt

This is another of those "visual extravaganzas" that caterers just love to serve and diners faint and swoon over. The colors and flavors are super-dramatic and, best of all, it's so easy to prepare. If someone sends you a box of those marvelous Texas Ruby grapefruits, here's the way to show them to best advantage.

Rinse scallops and pat dry. Slice horizontally into thin disks. Place in plastic bag with lime juice, onion, hot pepper flakes and salt and press out trapped air. (You can substitute lemon juice for the lime juice but the flavor's not quite as interesting.) Seal bag, set in a container and refrigerate, turning occasionally, for 3 to 4 hours or overnight. Drain off and discard marinade. Add

3	tablespoons olive oil
2	fresh jalapeña chilies, thinly sliced
	fresh cilantro, salt and grated black pepper to taste

salad base

1	package fresh spinach, washed and trimmed
2	oranges
1	grapefruit, preferably red or pink
1	small red onion, sliced paper thin and separated into rings
1	small red pepper, thinly sliced into strips
3/4	cup walnuts, broken into coarse pieces

orange dressing

Combine in a jar:

>grated rind of 1 orange

- 1/4 cup orange juice
- 1/4 cup wine vinegar
- 2/3 cup fruity olive oil
- 1 small clove garlic, minced
- 1 tablespoon minced onion
- 1 teaspoon salt

Garnish: thin strips of red pepper, thin rings of red onion, walnuts

PRESENTATION Arrange spinach on large platter. Slice oranges and grapefruits into wheels, then into quarters. Tuck into spinach around edges and sprinkle on walnuts. Drain scallops, spoon into a small bowl, top with red pepper, and set bowl into center of spinach. Top salad with red onion and spoon orange dressing over greens. Grate black pepper over all.

"alligator tail" salad

SERVES FOUR

This chicken is a variation on a dish by Boston food writer Peggy Glass*. It was given its name by her children because the almond coating looks like alligator skin and the shapes of the pieces are distinctly tail-like. Adults love them just as much as children do.

9   cups mixed greens, including some finely shredded purple cabbage, grated raw carrot, and thinly sliced yellow pepper for color

1 1/2   pounds chicken breasts, skinless and boneless, cut in long thin strips

batter

2/3   cup flour

1/2   teaspoon salt

1/2   cup milk

1   egg

1/2   teaspoon *each* poultry seasoning and pepper

       dash nutmeg

1 1/2   cups sliced almonds

corn oil and butter for frying

Dust strips of chicken with a little flour then dip in batter and roll in almonds. Set aside 15 minutes. Saute "tails" over medium heat using half butter, half oil to a depth of 1/4 inch. When golden brown, drain on paper towels and keep warm.

*Peggy Glass *Home Cooking Sampler: Family Favorites from A to Z,* Prentiss Hall

honey-mustard vinaigrette

Whisk together:

1/4	cup honey
1/4	cup vinegar
2	teaspoons Dijon mustard
1/2	cup oil
1/2	teaspoon salt

PRESENTATION Slice tails crosswise, part way through, into 1-inch sections. Line plates with greens, drizzle with dressing and lay several "tails" on top. Serve with warm Potato Scones (see Go-Withs).

easy taco bowls

This is an easy variation of the deep fried tortilla bowls served in Mexican eateries. Restaurant chefs make them by dropping a tortilla into deep fat and pressing down on the center with a ladle to make a bowl shape. These baked tortilla bowls comes out just as crisp with fewer calories and no smoking up the kitchen.

12-inch flour tortillas
olive oil
salt

Generously spread both sides of tortillas with oil and sprinkle lightly with salt. Invert small oven-proof bowls on a cookie sheet and drape tortillas over each, stroking with hands to shape. Bake at 400° for 12 to 15 minutes or until tortillas are lightly browned and crisp.

hot taco salad

SERVES FOUR

1	pound lean ground beef
1	cup chopped onions
1	green pepper, chopped
1	tablespoon cumin
1	tablespoon chili powder
2	cloves garlic

Brown meat, add onions, peppers and spices and cook until onions are wilted. Add garlic and cook 3-4 minutes more. Turn heat to lowest setting and keep warm.

cheese sauce

1	pound jack cheese, cubed
1	10-ounce can whole tomatoes, drained
2	chopped bottled jalapeño peppers (or to taste)

Heat together the cheese and tomatoes, stirring to combine. Add peppers to taste.

1	head iceberg lettuce, shredded
5	scallions, minced
1	avocado, diced, sprinkled with lemon juice

Garnish: sour cream

PRESENTATION Line bottom of taco bowls with shredded lettuce, sprinkle hot meat mixture over lettuce, then add hot tomato-cheese sauce, top with minced scallions and cubed avocado. Garnish with a dollop of sour cream and serve immediately on lettuce-lined plates.

jícama black bean salad

For a vegetarian meal, use this to fill taco bowls (preceding page.) Top with a dollop of sour cream and shredded cheese – longhorn cheddar is a striking gold color.

Combine:

1	cucumber, diced
2	tomatoes, chopped
1	medium jícama, diced
2	scallions, minced
1/4	cup minced cilantro
1	can black beans, rinsed and drained
1	avocado, diced
1/4	cup lime juice
1/4	cup olive oil
	red pepper flakes, garlic powder and salt to taste

Mix together and chill for 30 minutes.

1	head iceberg lettuce, shredded

Garnish: sour cream, shredded longhorn cheddar, and lettuce leaves.

PRESENTATION On lettuce-covered plates, pile vegetable mixture into taco bowls lined with shredded lettuce and top with salsa. Add a dollop of sour cream and sprinkling of cheese.

fresh salsa

1	carrot, peeled
1	rib celery
1 - 2	fresh chilies, to taste
1	small onion
1	clove garlic
1/4	cup lemon or lime juice
1	1-pound can whole tomatoes
1/4	cup chopped cilantro
	salt to taste

Process all until finely chopped.

Jícama. a brown root vegetable. is sometimes called the Mexican potato. It's flavor is sweeter, however, more like fresh water chestnuts, and its white flesh is very crisp. It goes equally well in savory mixtures, as here, and sweet fruit salads.

indonesian fruit & shrimp salad

This beautiful salad is served in a gorgeous leaf bowl that is surprisingly simple to create. Just line a shallow bowl with four or five large outer leaves of savoy cabbage and reserve the rest of the cabbage for another use.

The combination of ingredients is surprising too: papaya, cucumber, shrimp, orange, apple, hot peppers, cilantro, fish sauce, sesame oil and lime juice. In Thailand it's called yam chomphu, *in Java,* rudjak, *and it is served on ritual occasions. Everything can be assembled ahead of time, but add the cucumbers at the last minute because they tend to wilt in the dressing. Granny Smith apples stay crisp and don't discolor. The flavors of this dish are so stimulating and refreshing, I think it's the best light supper for a beastly hot day.*

2	Granny Smith apples, in 1/2-inch cubes (do not peel)
2	oranges, sectioned
1	cup pineapple cubes
1	papaya, cubed (save some seeds)
1	pound cooked, peeled large shrimp
1/2	English cucumber, halved lengthwise and sliced (do not peel)

cilantro lime dressing

1/4	cup minced cilantro
2	tablespoons fish sauce
1	tablespoon sesame oil
1/4	cup each sugar and lime juice
	fresh minced jalapeño chili or red pepper flakes to taste

Pour dressing over fruit-shrimp mixture,
 stir gently and refrigerate until well chilled.

**Garnish: thin threads of red cabbage (or radicchio,) large outer
leaves of savoy cabbage**

PRESENTATION Line a shallow bowl with several large outer
leaves of Savoy cabbage. Add sliced cucumber to fruit mixture just before
serving, toss gently to coat and scoop mixture into the leaf-lined bowl.

tropical grilled seafood salad

SERVES FOUR

8	bamboo skewers soaked in water for 10 minutes
1	pound large shrimp, cleaned, tails on
1	pound sea scallops
1	pound squid, sliced in 1-inch rings, tentacles whole

marinade

Combine:

3	cloves garlic, mashed.
3/4	teaspoon dried hot pepper flakes
1/3	cup peanut oil

1	avocado, sliced
1	mango, sliced
1	papaya, sliced
1	head lettuce, thinly shredded

In separate bowls coat shrimp, scallops and squid with 1/3 of oil, garlic and hot pepper marinade. Thread seafood on skewers and grill close to heat source, cooking about 4 to 5 minutes or just until shrimp turn pink and scallops and squid are opaque. Remove from heat and set aside to cool.

lime dressing

Combine:

	juice of 2 limes
2	tablespoons *each* peanut oil and soy sauce

PRESENTATION Make a nest of shredded lettuce and fill with grilled seafood, spooning any accumulated juices over lettuce. Arrange slices of fruit and avocado around sides and dribble with lime dressing. Serve at room temperature.

layered taco salad

SERVES SIX

Layered in a deep, clear glass bowl or composed on a large platter this salad is as beautiful as it is delicious. It's a complete meal and can be made strictly vegetarian by omitting the chicken. Bottled or fresh homemade salsa (see Salsas) completes the picture.

bean medley

Mix together and chill:

2	cans (15-ounce size) black beans, drained and rinsed
1/3	cup minced red onion
1/4	cup lemon juice
3	tablespoons olive oil
1/2	teaspoon cumin
	pinch cinnamon
	dried red pepper flakes to taste

2	large ripe tomatoes, coarsely chopped
1	large avocado, diced and sprinkled with lemon juice
1	bag thin restaurant style tortilla chips, lightly crushed
1	cup grated Monterey Jack cheese or longhorn cheddar
1	small head iceberg lettuce, shredded
1	cup shredded cooked chicken, optional

Top with

1	8-ounce carton "lite" sour cream

PRESENTATION In clear glass bowl or large platter alternate bean medley with layers of tomato, avocado, chips, cheese, lettuce and chicken, if used. Top with dollops of sour cream. Serve salad with salsa on the side. I like to add a big plate of piping hot Quesadillas (see Go-Withs.)

gravlax plate

SERVES EIGHT

There is a special elegance and mystery associated with this Scandinavian dish that is out of proportion to the simplicity of its preparation. Its history is said to go back to the Vikings when salmon was preserved with sugar, salt, pepper and dill and buried under a snow bank. Although today a refrigerator replaces the snow bank, the name gravlax, literally "grave salmon," survives.

The texture of the cured fish is like nothing else — meltingly smooth and delicate; a thin, pink, translucent sliver melts on the tongue. The flavor is slightly sweet, faintly salty, with a refreshing hint of herbiness provided by the dill — more the taste of the ocean itself than of fish.

Gravlax is considered a special-occasion delicacy in Scandinavia. Families pride themselves as having just the right technique for preparing and serving it, just as Americans have family traditions for the Thanksgiving turkey.

Americans, however, generally enjoy gravlax, not at home, but in fancy restaurants, which is too bad because the preparation of gravlax is one of those rituals, like making bread, that is especially satisfying.

The other foods that accompany gravlax are strictly dictated by tradition: parslied boiled potatoes or creamy potato salad, marinated cucumber salad, thinly sliced black bread or flatbread, and to drink, icy-cold aquavit or vodka. A chaser of premium ale is optional. Mustard-dill sauce and wedges of lemon, however, are mandatory. The pink potato salad in this version is a twist on tradition but not a break.

gravlax

Salmon comes in many shades. Some is pinky-beige rather than rosy-red. Ask your fish vendor to help you choose the reddest fish. It must be immaculately fresh (not previously frozen) so be sure that it was delivered that day.

3	pounds center-cut fresh salmon, cleaned, scaled, and deboned into 2 fillets
3	tablespoons aquavit or vodka
1/4	cup sugar
1/4	cup coarse salt
2	tablespoons white peppercorns, whirled in processor until coarsely cracked
1	cup fresh dill, coarsely chopped

gravlax sauce

2	tablespoons sugar
4	tablespoons Dijon mustard
3	tablespoons cream
1	tablespoon minced fresh dill

At least 2 (but no more than 3) days before serving, place the fillets skin-side down on a tray and rub aquavit or vodka into the flesh with your fingers. Sprinkle on salt, sugar and peppercorns and rub in. Spread dill evenly over both fillets and place one fillet on top of other, skin side up. Slide fish into large, clear plastic bag and close with a twist-tie. Lay fish in a pan, place a platter on top of fish and weight down with several heavy cans. Refrigerate for 2 to 3 days, turning morning and night.

When ready to serve, scrape away the curing mixture and pat fish dry. Set fillet on a board and, using a very sharp knife, cut thin slices holding the knife at an angle to the board.

Serve with potato and cucumber salads, next page.

gravlax plate

cucumber salad

1	long English cucumber
1/4	cup *each* white vinegar and water
2	tablespoons sugar
1	teaspoon salt
	pinch white pepper

Slice cucumber as thin as possible. (A mandoline makes paper thin slices easier to accomplish.) Combine with remaining ingredients and chill several hours or overnight. Drain before serving.

creamy pink potato salad

Thin-skin potatoes, both red-skin and light brown, have a creamy, waxy texture that's perfect for this recipe. The minced beets give this potato salad a beautiful, rosy hue.

9	cups sliced, cooked potatoes
3/4	cup minced celery
6	minced scallions
1/2	cup mayonnaise
1/4	cup white vinegar
1	cup sour cream
1/4	cup minced prepared pickled beets
	salt, pepper, minced fresh dill to taste

Garnish: lettuce (Boston, or other tender variety,) capers, lemon wedges, thin black bread or rye crisps

PRESENTATION   Arrange slices of salmon, loosely curled, on plates. Add a few leaves of lettuce topped with a scoop of potato salad and drained marinated cucumbers. Sprinkle potato salad with capers and tuck a wedge of lemon along side the fish. Serve with thin rye flatbread or the blackest, grainiest bread you can find. Some supermarkets carry a square, dark, imported loaf that's a perfect accompaniment.

These recipes are included because people often need a little something to **GO WITH** their salad. Some folks don't feel properly fed with just a salad. And that's fine because salads welcome so many interesting additions: breads of all kinds, a slice of quiche, a great soup, assorted appetizers, egg dishes, chicken wings... the list could go on and on. It has occurred to me as I choose my favorites that these extras may just steal the show from the stars. Here are some favorites from A (Alsatian Cottage Cheese Spread) to Z (Zucchini Pie.)

too-cooked wings

You won't believe these until you try them. This recipe produces the crunchiest wings ever. Men and children love them and are never embarrassed by the mountain of bones on their plates that reveals how many they've consumed. There are only three ingredients.

Any amount of wings, usually about 4 to 6 per person except for men and teenagers. Rinse wings, check for feathers and drain. While wet shake in a bag with flour to coat. Lay wings, not touching, on a shallow baking pan lined with oiled foil. Sprinkle generously with Seasoned Salt (I prefer Lawry's) and bake at 400° for one hour or until wings are a rich golden brown (no need to turn.) I like them best when they're dark brown. Remove to paper towels to drain. These are so crisp that you can eat the whole tip joint. Serve hot or cold.

surprise stuffed potatoes

SERVES FOUR

I'd be hesitant to include this recipe except for the fact I am always asked for it whenever I serve these potatoes. I say hesitant because recipes that include canned soups, so much the rage with our mothers' generation, are very unfashionable in today's trendy food circles. It's dishes like this that will bring a revival of those homey old recipes some day. The creamed spinach under a layer of fluffy potato is a neat surprise. You can use frozen broccoli instead of spinach for a change.

4	Idaho potatoes, baked
1/3	cup milk or more as needed
2	tablespoons butter
	onion powder, salt and pepper to taste

Halve potatoes, scoop out centers and prepare as for mashed potatoes. Set aside.

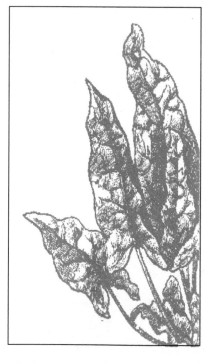

Combine:

1	package frozen spinach, thawed and squeezed dry
1	can cream of mushroom soup
1/2	teaspoon onion powder
1/4	teaspoon garlic powder
1/4	cup *each* sour cream and grated Parmesan cheese

Garnish: shredded cheddar cheese

Spoon spinach mixture into bottoms of potato skins and pile mashed potato mixture on top. Smooth tops making a crevice down center. Sprinkle with paprika. Bake for 1/2 hour in 400° oven. During last 5 minutes fill crevice with grated cheddar and heat until melted.

potatoes caroline

SERVES THREE
(or 2 teenagers); increase as needed.

3	large Idaho potatoes
1/4	cup olive oil
2	cloves garlic, mashed

Using a mandoline, slice potatoes, skins on, paper thin. Spread slices on a brown paper bag to drain. Blot well with paper towels. Tip: Thorough blotting is the secret to crispness. Mix oil and garlic. Cover the bottom of two jelly roll pans with a thin coat of oil. Place a layer of overlapping potato slices across one end. Add another row, overlapping first row. Continue until all potatoes are used up. Potatoes must not be more than three or four layers deep. Dribble remaining oil on top and bake at 400°, 35 to 45 minutes or until entire pan is rich golden brown and crisp. Tear into serving size pieces, blot excess oil with paper towels, sprinkle with coarse salt and serve piping hot.

variation

Sprinkle potatoes with paper-thin curls of onion rings, rosemary and cracked black pepper. Bake as above.

I guarantee this recipe will make your reputation as a cook. It's based on the classic Potatoes Anna, a 1-inch thick pancake of layered sliced potatoes dotted with butter and baked until soft in the center and golden brown outside. Yum! But never so Yum! as Potatoes Caroline. Humility aside, this is an improvement on perfection: There's no cholesterol because there's no butter. You get the intoxicating scent and nutty flavor of roasted garlic and just the best part: the crispy, crunchy, golden brown crust. People who cook for a living often say they don't eat their own cooking because they're tired of it by the time they serve it. I've always been that way myself. However, I have been known to eat the equivalent of two large potatoes-worth of this dish in a sitting. This recipe is the best reason in the world to get yourself a mandoline (an inexpensive slicing gadget available in kitchen stores.) The potato slices should be transparently thin, hard to do with a knife. Here are the proportions; you don't need a rigid recipe.

alsatian cottage cheese spread

Lots of flavor, low on calories.

2   cups dry curd cottage cheese, pureed

1/2   cup "lite" sour cream or yogurt

2   tablespoons *each* minced parsley, minced scallions, olive oil, and white wine

1   clove garlic, mashed

1/2   teaspoon *each* salt and thyme

Chill overnight. Serve with very thin diet rye crackers.

baked cheese sandwiches

Easy, easy, good, good.

12   slices good white bread

2   tablespoons soft butter

2   cups (1/2 pound) grated sharp cheddar

1 1/3 cups milk

3   eggs

1/2   teaspoon salt, freshly ground pepper

1/2   teaspoons *each* dry mustard and onion powder

1   teaspoon Worcestershire sauce

Butter bread and place 6 slices in 12x8x2-inch baking dish. Sprinkle with cheese and top with remaining bread slices. Mix eggs, milk and seasonings and pour over bread. Let stand 1 hour or overnight. Bake at 350° for 40 minutes.

baby blueberry muffins

These are the best blueberry muffins ever. A summer isn't complete for me without these. Make them in small muffin tins lined with cupcake papers.

1 1/2 cups flour

1/2   cup sugar

2   teaspoons baking powder

1/2   teaspoon salt

1/4   cup butter or margarine

1   egg

1/2   cup milk

1   cup well drained fresh blueberries

Combine dry ingredients and pinch in shortening with your fingers. Make well in center and pour in milk. Drop egg into milk and stir with fork, then incorporate dry ingredients, stirring just until blended. Fold in blueberries. Fill muffin cups 2/3 full, sprinkle heavily with sugar and bake at 400° for 20 minutes.

cranberry muffins

Substitute 1 cup coarsely chopped cranberries and 1/3 cup chopped walnuts for blueberries.

behreg

This milk crust never fails but don't use it for fruit pies. It needs to absorb the melting butterfat in the cheese for best flavor. The amount of milk varies with the dryness of the flour. The cheese that oozes around the edges is the best part.

cheese filling

12	ounces muenster cheese, grated
3/4	cup grated sharp cheddar
8	ounces cream cheese
2/3	cup chopped parsley
2	eggs

Beat all ingredients until combined.

crust

3	cups flour
1/2	teaspoon salt
1 1/2	sticks margarine
3/4	cup (about) lukewarm milk

glaze: 1 egg mixed with 2 tablespoons water
sesame seed or black seed (available in Indian and Middle Eastern markets)

Combine margarine with dry ingredients by rubbing between your fingers until mixture resembles a fine meal. Add milk gradually, mixing with two fingers until dough holds together. Knead briefly. The dough should be the consistency of your ear lobe. Pinch off walnut-size balls of dough and roll out 6-inch circles on unfloured surface. Fill with cheese mixture and fold to make semi-circles. To crimp edges, hold turnover in one hand and, at even intervals, push up edge of dough with middle finger while simultaneously pinching edge of crust between thumb and index finger. Trim uneven edges. Place on cookie sheet, brush with egg glaze and sprinkle with sesame seed or black seed.* Bake at 400° for 25 minutes or until nicely browned.

*Black seed is also known as nigella and kalonji. About the size of a sesame seed and coal black, the flavor is pungent, almost like rosemary or thyme. You can find black seed in Middle Eastern or Indian markets

Behregs are delicious little cheese turnovers. Although they are a bit time-consuming I make them often. There are times when I get an absolute craving for them. This recipe was given to me by a friend's Armenian mother-in-law. They can be eaten hot or cold, but I always make a big batch and reheat what I need in a toaster oven at serving time. The crust is very different from traditional pie crust in that you don't have to worry about chilling the butter or handling the dough too much. Nor do you sprinkle your rolling surface with flour. Just roll on a smooth surface such as Formica or butcher block. The first one may stick, but the rest will do fine.

black pepper grits

The world is full of people (none of them Southerners) who swear they hate grits. But nobody doesn't like grits prepared this way, even damn Yankees.

3 1/2	cups water
3/4	cup grits
1/4	teaspoon salt
2	eggs
1	cup grated cheddar cheese (Kraft Cracker Barrel Extra Sharp preferred)
2	tablespoons butter or margarine
1/2	teaspoon onion powder
2-3	teaspoons coarsely ground black pepper
	dash hot pepper sauce

Combine grits, water and salt and bring to boil over high heat whisking frequently. Beat eggs in small bowl, mix in some of hot grits and whisk egg mixture back into pan. Add remaining ingredients, stirring to melt cheese. Pour into buttered casserole and bake for 30 to 40 minutes or until puffed and brown. To serve, spoon onto plates and pass the butter.

boston brown bread

I lived in Boston for twenty years before I tasted the famous Boston Brown Bread. Like the equally famous Boston Baked Beans, you never see it in Boston. I bought a loaf at a fair and fell in love with it. Though the recipe goes back more than a century, it's perfect for the health-conscious way we eat today. Because it's steamed, not baked, it's moister than ordinary bread even though it contains no fat.

1	cup rye flower
1	cup cornmeal
1	cup whole wheat flour
1	teaspoon *each* salt and soda
2	cups buttermilk
3/4	cup molasses
1	cup chopped raisins

Mix all ingredients and pour into 2 buttered coffee cans or oven-proof containers of similar size and shape. Cover tops with buttered aluminum foil and tie with string. Set cans on a trivet in a large pot filled with an inch or two of water and cover with a tight-fitting lid. Over low burner steam for 3 hours or until loaves test done. Cool completely before serving.

clams rockefeller

Use ramekins or scallop shells — tastes remarkably like the real Oysters Rockefeller.

1	6-ounce can minced clams
1	package frozen chopped spinach, thawed
1	clove garlic, minced
2/3	cup bread crumbs
2	tablespoons butter
2	scallions, minced
	dash Worcestershire
1	tablespoon anisette or Pernod
	hot pepper sauce to taste
	milk or cream to moisten
	Parmesan cheese for topping

Squeeze spinach very dry and add remaining ingredients. Add enough milk or cream to make mixture moist but not soggy. Pack into four ramekins, sprinkle with cheese and bake at 425° for 15 to 20 minutes.

tex-mex corn soup

My college-age son's favorite soup "in the whole world." It's gooooood!

2	tablespoons olive oil
1	teaspoon cumin
1	medium onion, finely chopped
1/2	teaspoon oregano
	hot peppers (fresh or bottled) to taste
1	28-ounce can whole tomatoes, coarsely puréed in processor
1	1-pound can cream style corn
1	11-ounce can whole kernel corn
1	cup half and half cream

Sauté onion, cumin, (and peppers, if fresh) in oil until onion is wilted. Add remaining ingredients and heat gently over low flame until piping hot.

deviled crab cakes

Baltimore is famous for its crab cakes. My family lived in Virginia when I was a child. On trips north to see my grandmother in Brooklyn a crab cake lunch in Baltimore was the high point of the long drive. This is the way I remember them — crunchy outside, moist and delicate inside. If you have Old Bay Seasoning (a brand of mixed spices) so much the better, though it is not essential.

1/2	pound fresh crabmeat
3	Saltine-type crackers, crushed
1	egg
1	teaspoon *each* Worcestershire sauce and horseradish
1/2	teaspoon *each* dry mustard and Old Bay Seasoning (optional)
1	tablespoon *each* finely minced scallion and parsley
	cayenne or hot sauce to taste
	Corn meal for coating

Lightly mix all ingredients and shape into patties. Don't worry if they tend to fall apart; they firm up while cooking. Coat patties generously with corn meal and fry in equal parts of butter and salad oil until golden brown. Serve with lemon wedges and tartar or cocktail sauce or a mixture of the two. Pass the hot sauce for those who like a bit more Hell-fire. I prefer Durkee's Louisiana Hot Sauce (formerly Frank's) to Tabasco. It has more pepper flavor and a bit less heat.

easy sticky wings

Two ingredients! I just love a simple recipe that tastes fabulous. People cannot tell what these are seasoned with. They smell heavenly in the oven. Allow several wings per person.

Lay chicken wings in one layer in a shallow baking pan lined with foil and dribble generously with Japanese soy sauce (I use Kikkoman.) Turn to coat all sides.

Bake at 400°, turning occasionally, for about one hour or until sauce is syrupy and wings are glazed a deep, rich brown. Serve hot or cold.

egg burritos

These and a salad are the perfect light Sunday supper.

1	clove garlic, mashed
1	tablespoon oil
1	can (1 pound) refried beans
1	can (4 ounces) green chilies
6	eggs
1	tablespoon butter
3/4	cup salsa
1/3	cup minced cilantro
6	flour tortillas
3/4	cup shredded Monterey Jack cheese
1	cup sour cream

Sauté garlic in oil until lightly browned. Add refried beans and chilies and heat gently. Divide mixture between 6 tortillas and spread in strip down center. Set tortillas on a cookie sheet, sprinkle with cheese and place in 375° oven to warm. Meanwhile, wipe pan and scramble eggs in butter until barely set. Top each warmed tortilla with scrambled egg, salsa and cilantro and roll up. Place seam side down on warm plates and add a dab of salsa and sour cream to garnish.

the perfect fish chowder

In the Boston area, there's a wildly successful chain of restaurants that goes by an odd (to anyone not from these parts) name: Legal Seafoods. Such a name is not meant to be the punch line of a lawyer joke. It originated in the early 1900s attached to an earlier family business. Surprisingly, in twenty years of patronizing this establishment in the company of both native Bostonians and out-of-towners, I have never heard anyone wonder about the origin of the restaurant's peculiar name. However, I have witnessed and participated in countless discussions on the subject of discovering the formula for Legal's most famous dish: Fish Chowder.

Legal's Fish Chowder is, without a doubt, the single best reason behind the restaurant's deserved success. It is indisputably The Best in the world. Very thick, pure white, rich, and delicate, it contains no lumps of potatoes, no little cubes of salt pork (found in almost every recipe for chowder) no chunks of carrot, celery or green pepper, no discernable onion or garlic flavor. In years of trying to reproduce its elusive creamy texture by using heavy cream I failed dismally. To my disappointment the Fish Chowder that appears in The Legal Seafoods Cookbook (Doubleday, 1988) has carrots and cheese in it and the recipe introduction states that it will not taste quite like Legal's because home cooks cannot reproduce the concentrated fish base used at the restaurant.

Over the years my search for the recipe continued. Until, until… one day I was browsing through my mother's extensive collection of cookbooks. Among them was The Old Boston Cooking-School Cook Book by Fannie Merritt Farmer. It contained a recipe for Halibut Soup, which was significant for what it did not have: No potatoes, no salt pork, no vegetables, no heavy cream. Could it be??? Interestingly, the date on the cook book is 1906 (about the time the original Legal Seafoods was founded.) Fannie Farmer's secret for a concentrated fish base: rub the cooked fish through a sieve.

The following recipe is based on Miss Fannie's and is the closest I've come to reproducing Legal's Fish Chowder. If this isn't it, you could certainly fool me. Although I suspect that one could use a variety of chowder fish — cod, cusk or haddock, for instance, I have been so pleased with halibut that I haven't bothered to try another variety.

3/4	pound halibut
2	cups milk
1	slice onion
3	tablespoons butter
1 1/2	tablespoons flour
1/2	teaspoon salt
	pinch white pepper

Scald the milk with the onion; let stand 5 minutes then discard onion. Poach the fish in the milk just until cooked through (5 to 6 minutes.) With slotted spoon lift out the fish. Rub butter and flour together with your fingers to make a paste and add to hot milk, whisking briskly over medium heat. In the processor, purée about two-thirds of the fish and stir into milk. Crumble remaining fish into chunks and add to pot. Season with salt and white pepper and heat through. Pass the black pepper grinder at the table.

the best oven-fried eggplant

Just about every recipe for eggplant tells you to salt the slices and allow them to "weep" to remove bitterness. I beg to disagree. Bitterness in eggplant may be caused by growing conditions or may be a characteristic of a particular variety. Salting does little to remove bitterness but it goes a long way toward assuring you of fried eggplant as dry and tough as shoe soles.

I serve fried eggplant to vegetarians because it is so satisfyingly meaty. Here's how to make thick, crunchy slices with a moist, creamy center. This version uses less oil than frying by the traditional method. There's no recipe, just a method.

Set up three shallow bowls: one containing flour, the second, an egg wash (1 egg beaten with 2/3 cup milk) and the third containing bread crumbs. For best results the breadcrumbs should be homemade from a good, crusty bread and be slightly coarse-textured. Coat a jelly roll pan with a scant 1/8-inch of olive oil.

Slice eggplant a bit over 1/2-inch thick. Dredge slices in flour, dunk both sides in egg wash, then coat with crumbs. Set the slices into the oiled pan as you make them. Dribble the tops with a bit more oil and bake the eggplant at 400° for 25 to 30 minutes, turning once, until the crust is golden brown.

You may season the breadcrumbs if you wish with Parmesan cheese, pepper or herbs but do NOT add salt before cooking. Salt the eggplant slices just before serving as salt draws moisture which softens the crunchy crumb crust.

gougere

A cheesy popover ring. Very pretty.

1	cup milk, scalded
1/4	cup butter or margarine
1	teaspoon salt
1	cup flour
4	eggs
1/4	pound Gruyere cheese, grated

Add butter and salt to hot milk in pan. Add flour all at once and cook over medium heat, stirring well until mixture forms a ball. Turn off heat and beat in eggs one at a time to make a stiff, glossy paste. Add cheese, reserving 2 tablespoons for topping. Spoon high mounds of mixture in a ring on buttered baking sheet leaving open center about 2-1/2 inches in diameter. Brush top with milk and sprinkle with reserved cheese. Bake at 375° for 45 minutes or until richly browned. Serve warm with butter.

java wings

These define the end of the spectrum of finger-lickin' chicken. You've never seen a richer, gooier mahogany glaze than this. The coffee helps to cut the sweetness of the molasses.

1 1/2	pounds chicken wings
3	tablespoons *each* soy sauce, brown sugar and peanut oil
1/2	cup molasses
3	cloves garlic, mashed
2	tablespoon grated fresh ginger
1	teaspoon instant coffee granules
2	tablespoons sherry

Line pan with aluminum foil and add all ingredients. Toss to coat wings. Bake 45 minutes at 375°, turning occasionally or until rich, deep brown.

marbled tea eggs

These are little works of art. I once had the idea of using beet juice to make marbled eggs. It didn't work. This is the traditional method using tea and soy sauce. I like to use small eggs for this when I can find them, just for a change.

8	tea bags
3	cups water
1/2	cup dark soy sauce
8	small eggs
1/2	teaspoon whole anise seed or 1 star anise
1	stick whole cinnamon

Place all in a pan and heat at medium setting. When water boils, cover tightly and remove from heat. Let stand 10 minutes. Remove eggs with slotted spoon reserving cooking liquid. Cover with cold water and let stand until cool, then gently tap each egg on countertop until shells are webbed with fine cracks. Do not peel. Return eggs to reserved liquid and simmer for 1/2 hour, adding water if needed to cover eggs. Turn off heat and allow eggs to cool in liquid. Peel carefully when ready to serve. Use whole as garnish with Asian dishes.

mexican chili-cheese puff

Delicious! An "impossible" Mexican quiche. Much more than the sum of its parts.

1	cup pitted California ripe black olives, sliced
1	cup grated Monterey Jack cheese
1/2	cup minced red pepper
1	can (4 ounces) chopped green chilies, drained
6	scallions, chopped
3	eggs
3/4	cup biscuit mix
1 1/2	cups milk

Place olives, pepper, cheese, chilies and scallions in bottom of buttered 9-inch pie plate. Combine eggs, biscuit mix and milk. Whisk until smooth. Pour into pie plate and bake at 400° for 30 minutes or until puffed and golden.

mile-high popovers

Popovers: Not a roll, not a bread, nor a pastry, really, but a chemical marvel whereby a simple batter of flour, milk, eggs, and butter is transformed into something astonishing — glorious, golden, crunchy, hollow "chefs' hats," culinary miracles that happen literally right before our eyes if we have a window in the oven door. For years, in a search of the highest of all popovers, I tried every recipe variation I came across. The ingredients were always the same but the pans, method and baking instructions differed. One version advised using a pre-heated cast iron pan, another Pyrex custard cups. One advised mixing the batter in a blender, another suggested letting the batter stand for an hour, another directed placing the pan in a cold oven, then turning the heat on, another promised that starting in a 425° oven then turning the heat off at the end would produce the highest popover. None of these methods produced towering popovers; in fact, they all turned out pretty much the same.

My neighbor's daughter discovered the secret of producing GIANT popovers: Forget about the instructions that ALWAYS tell you to fill the muffin cups two-thirds full. Instead, fill them almost to the top. But of course! This will indeed produce huge popovers, so to avoid crowding leave the center cups unfilled.

Beat together just until smooth:

1	**cup flour**
1/2	**teaspoon salt**
1	**cup milk**
2	**eggs**
1	**tablespoon melted butter**

With soft butter, heavily coat muffin cups. Fill to the brim. Bake for 35 to 45 minutes at 425° or until golden brown. When done, open oven door and quickly stab each popover at its base with a small knife to allow the steam to escape. Leave in oven 10 minutes more. For variety try adding curry powder or herbs to the batter.

dutch babies

This recipe has been a family favorite for many years. We make it for breakfast or fill it with sautéed apples flavored with a little brown sugar and cinnamon for dessert. The cheese version goes with light suppers in place of bread. Because it's in the popover family it rises and forms fantastical shapes.

3	eggs
1/2	cup milk
1/2	cup flour
1/2	teaspoon salt
3	tablespoons butter

Melt butter in a 10-inch cast iron skillet and set aside. With wire whisk, beat eggs just until yolk and white combines. Beat in flour and salt until most lumps are gone. Add milk, beating until batter is almost smooth. Add most of cheese and half the melted butter. Swirl remaining butter around skillet to coat bottom and sides, then add batter. Sprinkle with a little more cheese. Bake for 35 to 40 minutes at 400° or until well browned. Slice in wedges and serve hot with butter.

cheese babies

Add

1/4	cup grated Parmesan cheese

and prepare as above.

oatmeal bread

This quick bread is light yet substantial enough to round out a meal. It has a lovely flavor. Serve it with butter or cream cheese.

Stir together in this order just until combined:

1	cup oatmeal
1	cup evaporated milk
1	tablespoon vinegar
1	egg
2	tablespoons melted butter
1/2	cup brown sugar
1	cup flour
1	teaspoon *each* salt and soda
2/3	cup raisins

Do not beat this batter. Bake in a brownie pan at 350° for 25 to 30 minutes.

orange poppy seed scones

These are the lightest, loveliest scones in the world. A nice accompaniment to delicate dishes such as chicken, crab or fruit salads.

1 3/4	cups flour
3	tablespoons sugar
2 1/2	teaspoons baking powder
2	teaspoons grated orange peel
1/3	cup butter
1/2	cup currants
1/4	cup poppy seeds
1	egg, beaten
5	tablespoons cream or milk

Combine flour, sugar, baking powder and grated peel. Pinch in butter with your fingers until well combined. Add currants and poppy seeds. Add egg and cream and stir with two fingers until dough forms a ball. Turn dough onto lightly floured counter and knead 4 or 5 times. On a cookie sheet, pat dough into 9-inch circle and cut into 12 wedges. Sprinkle top heavily with sugar and bake 10 to 12 minutes at 400°. Serve hot with butter and honey.

polenta gnocchi

Many years ago when my family went to Italy we ordered this dish every time we found it on a menu.

1	cup cornmeal
2 3/4	cups water
1	teaspoon salt
1	tablespoon butter
1	egg

Whisk cornmeal and salt into cold water and then heat and cook until thick and smooth. Remove from heat. Add butter and egg whisking vigorously. Pour on cookie sheet and chill. Cut into squares or circles (with a cookie cutter) and lay in buttered pan overlapping. Dot with butter, sprinkle generously with Parmesan cheese and bake in a 425° oven for 20 to 25 minutes or until top is lightly browned and butter is bubbly. Serve hot.

popover pizza puff

Kids love this.

3/4	pound lean hamburger
1	large onion, chopped
1	15-ounce can whole tomatoes
1	teaspoon oregano
1 1/2	cups (8 ounces) grated mozzarella
2	eggs
1	cup milk
1	tablespoon olive oil
1	cup flour
1/4	teaspoon salt
1/2	cup grated Parmesan cheese

Brown meat and onion. Purée tomatoes slightly in processor and add with their juice and oregano to meat mixture. Simmer 10 minutes. Pour mixture into an oiled 10-inch pie pan and sprinkle with mozzarella. Beat eggs, milk and oil until foamy. Add flour and salt, beating until batter is smooth. Pour batter over meat filling, sprinkle with Parmesan and bake at 400° for 30 minutes or until puffed and golden. Serve hot.

potato blintzes

Blintzes are basically stuffed crêpes. Most people who know them think immediately of the cheese-filled kind. Good as those are (especially topped with blueberries), I like potato blintzes even better. This recipe produces an especially light and delicate crêpe because it contains no milk. I scoop out the centers of baked Idaho potatoes for the blintz filling.

As a second treat, cut the potato skins into squares and lay them on a sheet of foil, dot with butter, sprinkle with onion powder, Parmesan cheese, salt and pepper and crisp them in a toaster oven. I toss these on salads like croutons.

crêpes

3/4	cup flour
1/2	teaspoon salt
2	eggs
1	cup water

Lightly whisk all ingredients together — never mind if there are some lumps. Let batter stand 1/2 hour or more. Batter will thicken on standing. If necessary, thin with water to consistency of heavy cream. In 5- to 6-inch skillet or crepe pan, make crêpes, cooking on one side only until set on top and lightly browned on bottom. Place crêpes slightly overlapping on sheets of foil or waxed paper to cool.

filling

3	tablespoons minced onions
2	tablespoons butter
2 1/2	cups mashed baked potatoes
1	egg
	milk or cream to moisten
	salt and white pepper to taste

Sautée onion in butter until wilted. Combine all filling ingredients. To make blintzes, lay a crepe on the counter, browned side up, and place a dab of potato mixture in center. Fold bottom of crepe up, sides in and top down and turn package over. When all are filled, fry them a few at a time in a little vegetable oil (such as Wesson.) Do not be tempted to use butter; it burns before the crêpes are browned. Drain on paper towels. Serve hot with sour cream and apple sauce on the side. Can be made ahead and reheated in a toaster over.

A delicious variation: Sautée minced fresh shiitake mushrooms with the onion – 2 or 3 will be enough to impart a subtle flavor.

potato scones

1 1/2	cups leftover mashed potatoes
1	cup biscuit mix
1/2	teaspoon onion powder
2	tablespoons butter, melted

Combine potatoes, onion powder and biscuit mix. Do not add any other liquid. Mix until dough forms a ball then place on buttered cookie sheet and pat into a 1/3-inch thick rectangle. Cut into squares and separate slightly. Spread butter over top and bake at 400° for 20 minutes or until golden brown. Serve hot with butter.

quesadillas

These are so easy and simple; how can they be so good?

3	12-inch flour tortillas
1/4	cup finely minced onion
2/3	cup grated Monterey jack cheese with hot peppers
1/2	cup grated sharp cheddar

Put tortillas on cookie sheet and sprinkle each with onion and cheese. Bake at 400° just until cheese melts and tortillas are crisp (about 3 minutes.) Cut into wedges and serve immediately.

red eggs & pickled beets

2	bunches small beets
1/2	cup cider vinegar
1/4	cup sugar
1	cinnamon stick
6	whole cloves
1	teaspoon pickling spice
6	hard-boiled eggs

Boil beets until tender. Reserve 1/2 cup cooking liquid in pan. Skin and slice cooled beets into a deep bowl. Shell eggs and place in bowl. To beet juice in pan add remaining ingredients. Bring to a boil and pour over beets and eggs. Refrigerate for 2 or 3 days before serving. Use both eggs and beets as garnish.

senate cheese straws

Popular in the Senate dining room many years ago.

3/4	pound sharp cheddar cheese, grated
1	stick margarine
2 1/4	cups flour
1/4	teaspoon cayenne
1	teaspoon salt

Combine in processor to make a very stiff dough. Chill briefly. Roll out 1/4-inch thick and cut into 1/4-inch strips. Lay strips on ungreased cookie sheet giving each a couple of twists. Bake at 375° for 20 minutes or until golden brown.

spanish omelette

This omelette is as popular in Spain (and many other Spanish-speaking countries) as the hamburger is here. It is nothing like what goes by the name in this country. In spain, it is often served at room temperature cut into small squares as a "tapa" or canapé, with drinks. In my family it regularly appears in pie wedges accompanied by a big spinach salad tossed with chunks of tuna. There's no recipe, you make it "by feel."

Fry sliced potatoes in olive oil until browned (a non-stick pan cuts down on the amount of oil you need.) Add chopped onions, salt and pepper and continue cooking until onions are wilted. Scramble enough eggs to just cover the potatoes and season with salt and pepper. Pour eggs over potatoes and cook covered over medium heat until top is almost set. Place a platter on top of pan, flip omelette onto platter and slide omelette back into pan to brown other side. If desired, serve with a light tomato sauce (sautée a bit of garlic in olive oil, add chopped, whole canned tomatoes and basil and cook 1/2 hour.) Kids prefer ketchup.

spoon bread

Not a bread at all, really, more like a low soufflé. This is a delicious traditional Southern dish served in my family on most holidays. Because it's so easy it does not require a special occasion to justify making it.

1	**cup cornmeal**
2	**cups boiling water**
1/2	**teaspoon salt**
2	**tablespoons soft butter**
4	**eggs, beaten**
1	**cup cold milk**

Whisk cornmeal slowly into boiling salted water. Turn off heat and add butter, eggs and milk. Beat well. Pour into hot buttered, shallow baking dish. Bake 25 minutes at 400°. Serve immediately and pass the butter.

quickie yeast rolls
in-time-for-dinner

Nothing says "home" like the smell of baking bread — but who has time? You do. These tender rolls can be started from scratch an hour before dinner.

The secret of speedy yeast rolls is temperature. Yeast organisms grow fastest when the climate suits them. Have all ingredients warm to speed rising of the dough. How to be sure the liquid for dissolving the yeast is the proper temperature? Use your hand; the temperature you'd draw for bath water is what yeast likes, too. To avoid chilling the yeast, warm the egg in a cup of almost hot water for a minute or two. Measure the flour in a glass cup and heat it in the microwave for a minute or two until if feels warm, not hot, to the touch. If kitchen is cool, rolls can rise in warm oven. Preheat oven for 2 to 3 minutes, just enough to take the chill off. Turn off heat before putting rolls in to rise. When risen, remove rolls and raise heat to bake.

1	tablespoon sugar
1/2	cup lukewarm milk
1	egg
1	teaspoon salt
2	tablespoons melted butter or margarine
2 to 2 1/2	cups flour

Turn off heat. Dissolve yeast and sugar in warm milk. Stir in egg, salt, and butter. Add enough flour to make a moderately stiff dough. Shape into 16 balls and place in well-buttered muffin cups. Cover with a moist towel and set in oven to rise. Bake at 400° for 20 to 25 minutes. Serve hot.

honey-pecan quick rolls

Follow recipe at left. To dough add

1/2	teaspoon cinnamon

In bottom of each heavily-buttered muffin cup place

1	teaspoon *each* butter, light brown sugar, honey, and coarsely chopped pecans

Shape and bake as above. Let stand 1 minute then turn pan upside down on platter for several minutes. Serve warm.

zucchini pie

A biscuit mix crustless quiche. You can use Swiss or any kind of cheese you have on hand or even mix a couple odds and ends you want to use up.

2	cups thinly sliced zucchini
1/4	cup minced onion
1 1/2	cups shredded Swiss cheese
1 1/4	cups milk
3	eggs
3/4	cup biscuit mix
1	clove garlic, mashed
1/4	teaspoon nutmeg freshly grated black pepper

Butter a 9-inch pie plate. Add zucchini, cheese and onions and toss to mix. Combine milk, eggs, garlic, nutmeg and biscuit mix, whisking until smooth. Pour into plate, sprinkle with pepper and bake at 400° for 30 to 40 minutes or until well browned and puffed.

Throughout this book, each salad recipe includes its own dressing. Of course, you can use any of those dressings on innumerable other salads. Here are some dressings alone that I must include because they are so good. Use them on any salad — pasta, grains, legumes, greens, cold meats or fish — or any combination thereof. A fabulous dressing makes any combination special.

avocado tofu dressing

The tofu disappears in this pretty green dressing. Try this dribbled across a big platter of sliced red and yellow tomatoes.

1	ripe avocado, diced
1	8-ounce package soft tofu
3	tablespoons lemon juice
2	tablespoons minced chives or scallions
1/2	clove garlic
	salt to taste

Purée and chill for an hour before serving.

buttermilk ranch dressing

This dressing tastes like the commercial variety but fresher and better.

Whisk together:

3/4	cup buttermilk
2	tablespoons sour cream
1/4	cup mayonnaise
2	tablespoons lemon juice
1/2	teaspoon *each* salt and onion powder
1/4	teaspoon *each* garlic powder and white pepper

avocado ranch dressing

To above recipe add 1 cubed avocado, a dash of hot sauce and a pinch of cumin. Puree in a processor.

cheddar cheese dressing

Everybody knows blue cheese dressing; cheddar makes a similar dressing that's a bit milder.

Purée the following in a processor:

2	cups mayonnaise*
1	teaspoon *each* Dijon mustard and Worcestershire
1/2	teaspoon horseradish
1/4	cup lemon juice
1/4	pound grated sharp cheddar
2	scallions, chopped
	dash hot sauce

*Use part yogurt to cut calories

chutney dressing

Use this for chicken or seafood salad as well as greens.

1/4	cup wine vinegar
3	tablespoons chutney
1/2	teaspoon *each* salt, curry powder and garlic powder
2	tablespoons Dijon mustard
1	tablespoon sugar
2/3	cup salad oil

creamy french dressing

This is easy, surprisingly delicious and very delicate. Serve over Boston lettuce or other tender greens.

1	cup heavy cream
1/2	teaspoon *each* salt, sour salt, garlic powder and onion powder

Mix all together well and allow to stand to thicken.

cold bearnaise sauce

We usually associate Bearnaise sauce with hot dishes, but it is equally delicious cold. When my daughter got married, we served mesquite-grilled whole beef tenderloin. The rare meat was arranged in overlapping thin slices on a long platter and presented at room temperature with a bowl of Cold Bearnaise beside it. The guests went wild. Do not double or halve this recipe.

3	tablespoons white wine
2	tablespoons tarragon vinegar
1	tablespoon finely minced shallot or onion
1/2	teaspoon dry tarragon
	few grains cayenne

Simmer until reduced by half. Pour into blender container and add

1	tablespoon lemon juice
3	egg yolks
1/2	teaspoon salt
	dash white pepper

In microwave or on stove top heat until bubbling (do not brown)

1 1/2	sticks butter

Blend yolk mixture for 3 to 4 seconds on high speed then begin pouring hot butter in a slow, steady stream. When butter is added, continue blending for 4 to 5 seconds. Scrape mixture into small bowl and set aside to cool. Whisk 1/4 to 1/3 cup sour cream into cooled mixture and place in refrigerator until ready to serve. Keeps well.

lime peanut butter dressing

Serve over cold grilled meats or fish.

1/3	cup *each* lime juice and peanut oil
1	tablespoon Thai fish sauce or soy sauce
1	tablespoon sugar
1	clove garlic, minced
2	tablespoons peanut butter
1/2	teaspoon red pepper flakes

Place all in processor and whirl to combine.

the best russian dressing

Use this on cold meats or as a sandwich spread.

1/2	cup mayonnaise
1/2	cup ketchup
1/4	cup sweet pepper relish
2	tablespoons horseradish
1	tablespoon brown mustard
1/2	teaspoon onion powder
	dash hot sauce

sauce gribiche

Serve with cold meats, chicken or seafood.

Whirl in processor:

2	hard-boiled egg yolks
1	teaspoon Dijon mustard
1/4	teaspoon white pepper
1	cup mayonnaise

Dribble in 1/4 cup wine vinegar. Spoon into bowl and fold in:

1/3	cup chopped dill pickles
1/4	cup minced parsley
2	tablespoons chives
1	teaspoon tarragon

vietnamese dressing

Use on a mixture of sprouts, grated carrot, turnip and radish, minced scallion and shredded Chinese cabbage.

1/3	cup *each* light soy sauce, lemon juice, brown sugar and peanut oil
1	tablespoon horseradish or wasabi powder
1/4	teaspoon hot oil
1/4	teaspoon black pepper
1/8	teaspoon five-spice powder

a word about sweet salad dressings

My Spanish grandmother had only one salad dressing in her otherwise extensive culinary repertory and it was absolutely delicious. It was a simple vinaigrette. She never measured, of course, so no one in the family was able to reproduce it consistently, or so we all said. She used three, not two, parts of oil to one part of vinegar, seasoned the wooden salad bowl with a clove of garlic mashed in salt (no pepper, no mustard) and sugar. I think my grandmother used about 2 to 3 teaspoons of sugar for each 1/4 cup of cider vinegar and 3/4 cup of olive oil. It was the faint trace of sweetness that made the dressing so delicious. Oddly, I don't believe I have ever seen a simple vinaigrette dressing containing sugar in any cookbook or food magazine.

Knowing how that sweet/sour combination compliments greens I have made a point of collecting a variety of sweetened dressings over the years. Often this type contains seeds of some sort — such as honey-mustard dressing which employs mustard seed either in dry powdered form or prepared. Mustard seed has the property of helping to emulsify the oil and vinegar. Celery seed and poppy seeds do the same, especially when you whirl the dressing in a processor to bruise the seed's hulls a bit.

american-style "french" dressing

This makes a mild, red, sweet and sour dressing that bears no resemblance to any authentic French dressing I've ever tasted. However, because of its color, it is strongly reminiscent of commercial pseudo-French dressings, only much, much better. Don't be put off by the canned soup; people will ask you for the recipe again and again.

Whisk together:

1	can tomato soup, undiluted
3/4	cup *each* vinegar and sugar
1	cup salad oil
1/2	teaspoon *each* garlic powder and onion powder
1	teaspoon salt

Chill before using.

catalina dressing

The card in my recipe file bearing this recipe has one word penciled in the margin: "Excellent."

Whirl in processor:

3/4	cup *each* vinegar and salad oil
1	cup powdered sugar
4	tablespoons tomato sauce or ketchup
1	teaspoon celery salt
1	teaspoon onion powder
1	clove garlic
1/2	teaspoon salt

blue ship tea room dressing

Many years ago there was a romantic little restaurant called the Blue Ship Tea Room which perched at the end of a long pier in Boston Harbor. A friend of mine who had moved to Florida phoned and asked if I could get the recipe for the restaurant's sweet house dressing which had been her favorite. I wrote to the Boston Globe which ran a daily readers' swap section called the "Chatter Page." My letter asking if any reader knew the recipe was soon published and several weeks later I received an anonymous envelope with a recipe and this note:

> I was given this recipe in strictest confidence. I have been pretty faithful about my oath of secrecy; in four years, I have only passed the recipe on twice!

This is a delicious dressing — just the right combination of sweet and sour.

Whirl in processor:

1/2	cup sugar
1/4	cup vinegar
1 1/3	cups salad oil
1	teaspoon salt
1	tablespoon *each* dry mustard and minced onion
3	tablespoons celery seed

Serve over a simple green salad with a bit of shredded carrot and red cabbage added for color.

cumberland dressing

Serve over cold turkey or chicken

3	tablespoons lemon juice
2	tablespoon *each* red currant jelly and heavy cream, melted together
1/2	teaspoon salt
1/2	cup salad oil
	pinch grated lemon rind

honey-poppy seed dressing

Purée all in processor:

1/2	cup honey
1/2	teaspoon salt
1/3	cup vinegar
1	teaspoon Dijon mustard
1	cup salad oil
2	tablespoons chopped onion
2	tablespoons poppy seeds

sour cream cooked dressing

Serve on chicken or fruit salad.

1/4	cup sugar
1	tablespoon flour
1/2	teaspoon *each* dry mustard and salt
2	eggs
1/2	cup sour cream
3	tablespoons white vinegar
1/2	cup heavy cream, whipped

Mix sugar, flour, mustard and salt in small heavy pan. Add eggs, sour cream and vinegar. Set pan over low heat and whisk mixture continuously until thickened. Chill. At serving time fold in 1/2 cup whipped cream or an additional 1/2 cup of sour cream.

salsa and its cousins from all over the world

Salsas have become the "in" thing recently, but the idea is hardly new. Just about every nationality has, as part of its traditional cuisine, some uncooked accompaniment or topping made quickly from fresh ingredients whose purpose is to add excitement and bite to plainer fare.

These toppings can be very useful. At our house, whenever we grill food over coals, there is usually plenty of cooking time left in the fire after dinner comes off. So that the coals don't go to waste, we throw on chicken breasts, lamb chops, sirloin tips, skewered shrimp, or marinated vegetables. This second meal goes into the fridge to re-emerge the next evening served with one of these toppings.

banana chutney

Toss large shrimp with curry powder and a little oil and grill over very hot coals just until pink. Serve cold with this exotic Indian relish.

1/8	cup lemon juice
2	bananas, diced
1/4	cup minced scallions
1/4	cup chopped peanuts
	pinch salt

Mix just before serving.

black bean salsa

For any grilled poultry, fish or meat.

1	1-pound can black beans, drained
	grated peel of 1 orange
1	cup chopped orange pulp
1	tomato, seeded and chopped
2	jalapeño chilies, minced
1/4	cup lime juice
1/4	cup olive oil
1	avocado, peeled and chopped
1/2	cup cilantro, minced

Combine all but last two ingredients and chill well. Just before serving add avocado and cilantro. Add salt to taste.

carrot raita

Light and tangy, this is an Indian relish.

1	large carrot, grated
1 1/2	cups yogurt
1/4	teaspoon salt
1	tablespoon minced coriander leaves
	red pepper flakes to taste
	pinch cumin

Mix together and chill well

filipino radish & orange salsa

Nice on grilled pork.

1   cup chopped red radishes or daikon
1   cup chopped orange pulp
1   cup chopped ripe tomatoes
1/4 cup *each* sugar and vinegar
1/2 teaspoon salt

fresh mango chutney

1 1/2 cups mango, chopped
2   tablespoons lime juice
1   tablespoon *each* grated lime rind and grated ginger
1/4 cup minced red onion
4   tablespoons minced cilantro
1   teaspoon sugar
     hot pepper flakes and salt to taste

Combine and chill.

hawaiian pineapple-tomato salsa

Good for grilled tuna, swordfish, shark or mahi mahi.

2   cups fresh pineapple, chopped
1   cup seeded, diced tomatoes, preferably a yellow variety
2   tablespoons minced scallion
2   tablespoons *each* lemon juice and ketchup
1/4 cup cream
     Salt and pepper to taste.

Combine all and chill well.

japanese turnip relish

Serve on grilled swordfish, tuna or chicken.

2   cups grated turnip
1/2 cup grated mild onion or minced scallion
1/4 cup *each* white vinegar, lemon juice, prepared horseradish
3   tablespoons sugar
3/4 teaspoon salt

Combine and chill well.

mock kim chee

Tangy, fiery kim chee is served at every Korean table to lend bite to any dish. It is traditionally made with fermented cabbage, garlic and hot peppers. This is a milder version that doesn't need to stand for days to ferment.

1   cup coarsely grated turnip
1   clove garlic, mashed
1   teaspoon grated fresh ginger
1/2 cup water
1   teaspoon salt
1   teaspoon dried red pepper flakes
1/2 cup water

Combine all and chill overnight.

pineapple-mint chow chow

Serve on cold grilled lamb or chicken.

3	cups crushed pineapple, canned or fresh
1	large English cucumber, halved and sliced
1/4	cup *each* minced fresh mint and scallions
1	teaspoon salt
1	clove garlic, crushed
1/2	teaspoon hot red pepper flakes
2	tablespoons white vinegar
2	tablespoons sugar

Combine cucumber, scallions and salt and allow to stand 1/2 hour. Pour off accumulated liquid and drain well. Add remaining ingredients and chill well.

papaya jícama salsa

This is another super crunchy salsa, thanks to the jícama.

2	papayas, cubed
1 - 2	green chilies
1/2	cup chopped red onion
1	clove garlic
1/4	cup cilantro
1	teaspoon grated lime peel
1/2	cup lemon or lime juice
2	tablespoons olive oil
1	cup jícama

Process until roughly chopped.

pico de gallo (rooster's beak)

This crunchy, tangy relish comes from south of the border and there are as many variations as there are cooks.

1/2	pound jícama, cut in chunks
2	oranges, peeled and sectioned
2	tablespoons lemon juice
	dried red pepper flakes
	salt to taste

Using short pulses, coarsely grind jícama and orange in processor. Season to taste with salt and red pepper and chill well.

tomato horseradish relish

Serve on cold meats or fish.

1 1/2	cups chopped, seeded tomatoes, drained
1/2	cup heavy cream
4	tablespoons horseradish
1/4	cup chopped parsley
1/4	cup mayonnaise
1	teaspoon paprika
2	tablespoon chopped chives or scallions.

popular thai sauces

In Thai restaurants peanut sauce and cucumber relish are always paired with the skewered chicken, beef or pork appetizer known as satay, but you can use these sauces with any grilled meats. Rub the meat with a mixture of cumin, turmeric, ginger and a little oil and grill.

Sweet red chili sauce often accompanies grilled whole chicken in Thai restaurants. Prepare split chickens as above and grill as usual.

cucumber relish

1/3	cup rice vinegar
3	tablespoons water
1/4	cup sugar
1/4	cup minced red onion
1	cup minced English cucumber (no seeds)
2	tablespoons minced cilantro
1	small chili, thinly sliced
1/2	teaspoon salt

Mix and chill to blend flavors.

peanut sauce

2	tablespoons oil
2	tablespoons grated onion
2	cloves garlic, mashed
2	fresh hot chilies, minced, or dried red pepper flakes to taste
2	tablespoons lemon juice
1	tablespoon fish sauce
1/2	cup crunchy peanut butter
2	teaspoons sugar
1	cup coconut milk

Cook onion and garlic in oil until wilted. Add remaining ingredients and simmer for a few minutes. Serve warm.

sweet red chili sauce

1/2	cup chopped fresh red chilies
3	cloves garlic, crushed
2	teaspoons fish sauce
1/3	cup lemon sauce
1/4	cup honey

Blanch garlic in boiling water for 2 minutes. Grind all ingredients in processor until smooth.

NO KIDDING:
how to boil an egg!

If you are using hard boiled eggs as a garnish, you want them to look their best.

Eggs are frequently found in the company of salads — in the dressing (Caesar), as part of the composition (Nicoise) or in egg salad itself. Hard boiled eggs can brighten up a plate, sliced in wedges or bull's eyes, or sieved over marinated asparagus or green beans.

Boiling a good-looking egg requires more care than is usually given to this humble project. You don't want the egg's shell to crack in cooking or the white to tear apart when you try to remove the shell. The yolk of a perfect hard-boiled egg is cooked through with no gray-green velvet around it.

Here are a few tips for perfect hard boiled eggs. Tip 1: Starting eggs in cold water prevents cracking. (Some people pierce one end of the shell with a pin for the same purpose.) Tip 2: Eggs that are older than a week peel more easily than very fresh eggs. (To tell the difference remember this: Older eggs stand on end in water, young eggs lie on their sides.) Tip 3: You can avoid damaging the whites by shelling the egg under water, getting your finger tips gently under the thin membrane that lines the shell.

Place large eggs in a pan with cold water to cover by about 1 inch. Heat without a cover, watching for the first large bubbles to rise to the surface. Reduce heat to keep water just below boiling point and begin timing exactly 10 minutes. Gently turning eggs occasionally helps to keep yolk centered. At 10 minutes, remove one egg and quickly shell it under cold running water. Check yolk. If cooked through, remove remaining eggs and flush with cold water to stop cooking. If not, cook a minute or two more.

COOKING FISH

Most recipes tell you to cook fish till it flakes. Actually, fish that flakes may be dry and overcooked. Instead, cook fish just until the flesh at the center becomes opaque, usually at 165° on a thermometer.

broiling Preheat broiler very hot. Brush fish with butter or oil, season with salt and pepper. Broil without turning just until cooked through, about 9 minutes per inch of thickness.

poaching Use enough poaching liquid to completely immerse fish. There are many recipes for poaching liquid but a fish or chicken bouillon cube dissolved in water and white wine works as well as most. Bring liquid to a boil, immediately reduce heat to lowest setting and place fish in pan. Cover tightly and cook gently until fish is opaque at thickest part, testing often. Allow 6 to 8 minutes per pound of fish or 10 minutes per inch of thickness.

HOW TO POACH CHICKEN

When a recipe calls for cooked chicken breasts, this easy method results in moist and tender morsels every time. No need to fear overcooking either.

4	cups water
1	carrot, sliced
1/4	cup sliced onion
	a few sprigs parsley
1	pair whole chicken breasts (with skin and bones)
2	chicken bouillon cubes

Combine all, cover and bring to a boil over high heat. Immediately turn off heat and let stand for two hours. Remove skin and bones and reserve broth for another use. Use in any recipe calling for cooked chicken breasts.

proper internal temperature is key to succulence

If you have trouble telling when the salmon fillets or chicken cutlets are done the best way is to check the internal temperature with a thermometer. You can use a conventional thermometer that stays in the meat during cooking or the instant-read variety that you stab into the thickest portion at around the end of the cooking period.

beef
    rare .... 140°
    medium .... 160°
    well-done .... 170°

veal .... 170°

lamb
    medium-rare ...... 140° to 150°
    well-done .... 170°

ham, fully cooked ... 130° to 140°

pork .... 155° to 165°

fish .... 165°

chicken .... 165°

turkey cutlets .... 170°

ABOUT GRILLING

The charcoal we grill with today is virtually flavorless. Charcoal itself provides no more flavor than an electric coil in a broiler unless we add additional flavoring chips, such as mesquite or hickory.

Grilling and broiling differ in only one aspect: the location of the heat source. But therein lies the essence of why foods cooked by the former method taste so much better than those by the latter.

In broiling the heat is on top; in grilling the heat is below. The significance of that point is this: The rich, grilled flavor that we love in everything from hotdogs to sirloins to grilled vegetables comes from smoke. Both broiling and grilling burn particles of fat, but in broiling the resulting smoke rises off the surface of the foods and into the air. In grilling, fats drip down onto the heat source and vaporize to become smoke which then rises from below. As it passes through the foods on its way heavenward, it bastes all food surfaces and leaves behind that wonderful grilled flavor we all recognize.

But where exactly does that taste come from? It comes primarily from the burning of fat contained in the juices dripping down on the heat source. It matters not whether the heat is derived from gas, electric or coals. And it matters not whether the fat is animal (such as marbling in a steak,) or vegetable (such as the olive oil in grilled mushrooms.) When *any* fat hits *any* fire the flavor imparted by the resulting smoke is pretty much the same. Therefore, to increase the smoky, grilled flavor of any dish, use a marinating or basting mixture containing plenty of oil or fat. Calories? Don't worry. They're mostly burned off in the cooking.